The Ancient History of China

Sheila Hollihan-Elliot

MC Mason Crest
Philadelphia

CHINa
THE EMERGING SUPERPOWER

The Ancient History of China

Sheila Hollihan-Elliot

Mason Crest
Philadelphia

Mason Crest
370 Reed Road
Broomall, PA 19008
www.masoncrest.com

Copyright © 2013 by Mason Crest, an imprint of National Highlights, Inc.
All rights reserved.
Printed and bound in the United States of America.

CPSIA Compliance Information: Batch #CH2013-1.
For further information, contact Mason Crest at 1-866-MCP-Book.

First printing

1 3 5 7 9 8 6 4 2

Library of Congress Cataloging-in-Publication Data

Hollihan-Elliot, Sheila.
  The ancient history of China / Sheila Hollihan-Elliot.
    p. cm. — (China: the emerging superpower)
  Includes bibliographical references and index.
  ISBN 978-1-4222-2154-9 (hardcover)
  ISBN 978-1-4222-2165-5 (pbk.)
  ISBN 978-1-4222-9443-7 (ebook)
  1. China—History—To 221 B.C.—Juvenile literature. 2. China—History—Qin dynasty, 221-207
B.C.—Juvenile literature. 3. China—History—Han dynasty, 202 B.C.-220 A.D.—Juvenile literature.
  I. Title.
  DS741.5.H65 2012
  931—dc22
                                   2010047757

Table of Contents

Introduction

Dr. Jianwei Wang
University of Wisconsin–Stevens Point

Before his first official visit to the United States in December 2003, Chinese premier Wen Jiabao granted a lengthy interview to the *Washington Post*. In that interview, he observed: "If I can speak very honestly and in a straightforward manner, I would say the understanding of China by some Americans is not as good as the Chinese people's understanding of the United States." Needless to say, Mr. Wen was making a sweeping generalization. From my personal experience and observation, some Americans understand China at least as well as some Chinese understand the United States. But overall there remains some truth in Mr. Wen's remarks. For example, if you visited a typical high school in China, you would probably find that students there know more about the United States than their American counterparts know about China. For one thing, most Chinese teenagers start learning English in high school, while only a very small fraction of American high school students will learn Chinese.

In a sense, the knowledge gap between Americans and Chinese about each other is understandable. For the Chinese, the United States is the most important foreign country, representing not just the most developed economy, unrivaled military might, and the most advanced science and technology, but also a very attractive political and value system, which many Chinese admire. But for Americans, China is merely one of many foreign countries. As citizens of the world's sole superpower, Americans naturally feel less compelled to learn from others. The Communist nature of the Chinese polity also gives many Americans pause. This gap of interest in and motivation to learn about the other side could be easily detected by the mere fact that every year tens of thousands of Chinese young men and women apply for a visa to study in the United States. Many of them decide to stay in this country. In comparison, many fewer Americans want to study in China, let alone live in that remote land.

Nevertheless, for better or worse, China is becoming more and more important to the United States, not just politically and economically, but also culturally. Most notably, the size of the Chinese population in the United States has increased steadily. China-made goods as well as Chinese food have become a part of most Americans' daily life. China is now the second-largest trade partner of the United States and will be a huge market for American goods and services. China is also one of the largest creditors, with about $1 trillion in U.S. government securities. Internationally China could either help or hinder American foreign policy in the United Nations, on issues ranging from North Korea to non-proliferation of weapons of mass destruction. In the last century, misperception of this vast country cost the United States dearly in the Korean War and the Vietnam War. On the issue of Taiwan, China and the United States may once again embark on a collision course if both sides are not careful in handling the dispute. Simply put, the state of U.S.-China relations may well shape the future not just for Americans and Chinese, but for the world at large as well.

The purpose of this series, therefore, is to help high school students form an accurate, comprehensive, and balanced understanding of China, past and present, good and bad, success and failure, potential and limit, and culture and state. At least three major images will emerge from various volumes in this series.

First is the image of traditional China. China has the longest continuous civilization in the world. Thousands of years of history produced a rich and sophisticated cultural heritage that still influences today's China. While this ancient civilization is admired and appreciated by many Chinese as well as foreigners, it can also be heavy baggage that makes progress in China difficult and often very costly. This could partially explain why China, once the most advanced country in the world, fell behind during modern times. Foreign encroachment and domestic trouble often plunged this ancient nation into turmoil and war. National rejuvenation and restoration of the historical greatness is still considered the most important mission for the Chinese people today.

Second is the image of Mao's China. The establishment of the People's Republic of China in 1949 marked a new era in this war-torn land. Initially the Communist regime was quite popular and achieved significant accomplishments by bringing order and stability back to Chinese society. When Mao declared that the "Chinese people stood up" at Tiananmen Square, "the sick man of East Asia" indeed reemerged on the world stage as a united and independent power. Unfortunately, Mao soon plunged the country into endless political campaigns that climaxed in the disastrous Cultural Revolution. China slipped further into political suppression, diplomatic isolation, economic backwardness, and cultural stagnation.

Third is the image of China under reform. Mao's era came to an abrupt end after his death in 1976. Guided by Deng Xiaoping's farsighted and courageous policy of reform and openness, China has experienced earth-shaking changes in the last quarter century. With the adoption of a market economy, in just two decades China transformed itself into a global economic powerhouse. China has also become a full-fledged member of the international community, as exemplified by its return to the United Nations and its accession to the World Trade Organization. Although China is far from being democratic as measured by Western standards, overall it is now a more humane place to live, and the Chinese people have begun to enjoy unprecedented freedom in a wide range of social domains.

These three images of China, strikingly different, are closely related with one another. A more sophisticated and balanced perception of China needs to take into consideration all three images and the process of their evolution from one to another, thus acknowledging the great progress China has made while being fully aware that it still has a long way to go. In my daily contact with Americans, I quite often find that their views of China are based on the image of traditional China and of China under Mao—they either discount or are unaware of the dramatic changes that have taken place. Hopefully this series will allow its readers to observe the following realities about China.

First, China is not black and white, but rather—like the United States—complex and full of contradictions. For such a vast country, one or two negative stories in the media often do not represent the whole picture. Surely the economic reforms have reduced many old problems, but they have also created many new problems. Not all of these problems, however, necessarily prove the guilt of the Communist system. Rather, they may be the result of the very reforms the government has been implementing and of the painful transition from one system to another. Those who would view China through a single lens will never fully grasp the complexity of that country.

Second, China is not static. Changes are taking place in China every day. Anyone who lived through Mao's period can attest to how big the changes have been. Every time I return to China, I discover something new. Some things have changed for the better, others for the worse. The point I want to make is that today's China is a very dynamic society. But the development in China has its own pace and logic. The momentum of changes comes largely from within rather than from without. Americans can facilitate but not dictate such changes.

Third, China is neither a paradise nor a hell. Economically China is still a developing country with a very low per capita GDP because of its huge population. As the Chinese premier put it, China may take another 100 years to catch up with the United States. China's political system remains authoritarian and can be repressive and arbitrary. Chinese people still do not have as much freedom as American people enjoy, particularly when it comes to expressing opposition to the government. So China is certainly not an ideal society, as its leaders used to believe (or at least declare). Yet the Chinese people as a whole are much better off today than they were 25 years ago, both economically and politically. Chinese authorities were fond of telling the Chinese people that Americans lived in an abyss of misery. Now every Chinese knows that this is nonsense. It is equally ridiculous to think of the Chinese in a similar way.

Finally, China is both different from and similar to the United States. It is true that the two countries differ greatly in terms of political and social systems and cultural tradition. But it is also true that China's program of reform and openness has made these two societies much more similar. China is largely imitating the United States in many aspects. One can easily detect the convergence of the two societies in terms of popular culture, values, and lifestyle by walking on the streets of Chinese cities like Shanghai. With ever-growing economic l interactions, the two countries have also y interdependent. That said, it is naïve to vill become another United States. Even if emocracy one day, these two great nations e to eye on many issues.

ancient civilization and a gigantic country vays a challenge. If this series kindles read- a and provides them with systematic infor- ful perspectives, thus assisting their forma- and realistic image of this fascinating coun- thors of this series will feel much rewarded.

This bronze figure of a horseman was created during the Han dynasty. Han rule, which began in 206 B.C. and lasted until A.D. 220, was interrupted from A.D. 9 to 23, when a reformer named Wang Mang held power in China.

The Chinese Way

The year was 3 B.C. As far as the eye could see, the road to the Han capital was filled with people from the far-off Shandong Peninsula. These were not wealthy people, but poor farmers and fishermen. Mothers trudged along, their crying children in tow. Hunger and thirst stalked the crowd. The lucky ones carried a bit of dried fish in their sacks. Any fruit or vegetables growing along the way were quickly grabbed and eaten—but furtively, as stealing food was a crime punished by flogging.

The weakest travelers succumbed to the hardships of the journey. Many of the dead could not be buried. Their corpses were simply abandoned in roadside ditches, where they lay amid the slop generated by the massive crowd—the overpowering stench of decaying flesh and waste rising in the hot sun. In the wayside villages, peasants heard the approach of the possessed mob and locked their town gates in fear, even though it was not yet night. What was happening?

The Mandate of Heaven

This was a new age of omens. Two years earlier, the Lord of the Red Essence had appeared to a poor provincial tutor and prophesied that the Han dynasty (whose official color was red) must come to an end unless morality was renewed. If the kingdom did not reform itself in a "new beginning," the Mandate of Heaven—the divinely bestowed right to rule—would be stripped from the Han. It was rumored that the sages were now busy studying the recently discovered "Ceremonies of Zhou" to learn the rituals and rules that should be in force to re-create the utopia of the past. The changes the overseers tried to keep from the people were sweeping: it was rumored that land was to be taken from the nobles and given to farmers, and that slaves would no longer be bought and sold. But that had not come to pass. The situation did not look good.

Everyone knew that Heaven took away the mandate to rule by first signaling the people with unexpected natural catastrophes. Whoever successfully fought for and gained the imperial seals after that signal was the new ruler chosen by Heaven. Turmoil and death were surely on the way.

But something wonderful happened. The wild woman of the Shandong shamans had just prophesied that the Queen Mother of the West, the goddess of longevity, would soon grant immortality to those who met her in Chang'an, the capital. No matter that the capital was more than 650 miles away. Death and turmoil would not harm those who had been granted immortality. So hordes of believers abandoned their boats, nets, farms, and villages and started the long trek west to Chang'an.

When the mob reached Chang'an, the guards opened the city gates because the Shandong peasants were not armed. Believers spoke of the Queen Mother and inquired if the tiger-toothed, leopard-tailed goddess had appeared yet. The answer was no, so the mob camped and waited. Days passed. Some Shandong believers suggested that the Queen Mother might be unaware of their presence, so they climbed on the rooftops, banged their drums, and shouted to summon the goddess. After several months of noise and disappointment, the pilgrims trudged back home, feeling that even the gods had abandoned them.

Several years later, a Confucian scholar, Wang Mang, was handed the rule from the Han. Wang Mang called his dynasty Xin, or New, referring to the omen that said there should be a new beginning. He sought to create the utopia that he believed had existed in the past. But Wang Mang did not seem to be favored by Heaven—it was even rumored that his supporters had faked the omens favoring his rule.

The gods sent floods. First the outflow of the Yellow River moved south of Shandong, killing people and livestock and destroying nearly all the villages in its new path. Two years later, the river moved to the north and destroyed the northern part of Shandong. Next, the dikes holding the middle part of the Yellow River in its banks broke, and the rich farms and villages in central China were swept away. Then Heaven reversed the torment and sent China five years of drought. Millions died of starvation. Survivors wandered, shocked and dazed, over the countryside. Many fled to the mountains and became bandits.

Retreating to his study to pore over the "Ceremonies of Zhou" for some insight that had eluded him in his previous studies, Wang Mang held onto his ideals. But in Shandong, disappointed peasants decided that they had been tricked—the Mandate of Heaven was not to be taken from the Han, but from the usurper Wang Mang. They painted their foreheads red, in respect for the Han dynasty, and started a new march on the capital. Han loyalists joined these "Red Eyebrows" along the route.

The Emperor Falls, but the Chinese Way Endures

Wang Mang's advisers begged him to fight the rebellious clans, who were now close to the capital. Wang Mang shouted his answer in a fit of frustration and rage: he ordered his armies to desecrate the temple built by the Han emperor Gao Zu, instructing the soldiers to whip the walls with the same whips used on criminals—to teach the malevolent gods a lesson. This supreme insult was too much for the rebels. The fault was not the gods', but Wang Mang's. They stormed the palace and found Wang Mang in his study, reciting from Confucius. With a swipe of the sword, a Red Eyebrow rebel beheaded Wang Mang and ended the quest for utopia.

Wang Mang's embryonic Xin dynasty had been destroyed. What

This illustration from a 17th-century Chinese book titled *Lives of the Emperors* shows a Han emperor with scholars translating classical texts. In Chinese culture, great emphasis has always been placed on studying the lessons of the past.

survived was much more important—"the Chinese Way," the essential culture and identity of the Chinese people.

This book presents the story of ancient China, its heroes, villains, ideas, and major events—which shaped the identity and actions of Chinese people for thousands of years. Even today, the epic tale of ancient China remains meaningful and continues to influence Chinese thought and activity, just as the Bible and the Qur'an (Koran) continue to inform the outlook of Jews, Christians, and Muslims. But the events and stories of ancient China do not form the basis of a religion; rather, they trace the growth of the Chinese Way. Even before attending school, every Chinese child learns about the country's distant past, because in the accounts of ancient China are contained the Chinese culture's fundamental lessons about how best to behave and prosper in the world.

Rice began to be grown in irrigated fields, like the one shown here, approximately 6,500 years ago. The labor-intensive nature of rice cultivation required a fairly complex, organized society.

The Seeds of Chinese Civilization

Around 10,000 B.C., at the end of the Ice Age, the Neolithic period in China began. Neolithic (from *neo*, meaning "new"; and *lithos*, "stone") refers to the last phase of the Stone Age, during which humans developed polished-stone tools and the nomadic hunting and gathering lifestyle that had characterized previous eras was gradually replaced by a more settled existence based on agriculture.

Neolithic culture reached its height in China from about 5000 to 2500 B.C. Tribes settling along the banks of the Yellow River in the north became the dominant influence on the future Chinese civilization. These tribes included peoples who would later be identified as the Xia, Shang, and Zhou clans. Yet their cultures adopted numerous ideas and skills from groups that settled along the Yangtze River Delta in southern

China, and from groups living even farther south, in what is today northern Vietnam.

The Development of Agriculture

As was the case elsewhere in the world, China's Neolithic cultures were complex and creative, despite their rudimentary technology. Essential cultural patterns for the next several thousand years were already emerging.

The great advance in Neolithic society was the domestication of plants and animals. In China agriculture first developed in two main regions—along the Yellow River valley in the north; and in the southeast, between the Yangtze River and the jungles of northern Vietnam and the China coast. In the north, millet, a small round grain, was the main foodstuff. Gourds, beans, and a few other simple garden plants were cultivated in the Yellow River region as well. Pigs were also raised for food.

Neolithic tribes followed the slash-and-burn system of agriculture: trees and brush were cut down and the land was then burned, making it easier to plow. Plowing had to be done by hand because no large draft animals were yet domesticated. Stone spades have been found that were undoubtedly used for the digging. After several years, when the fertility of the earth had been exhausted because the same crops were grown again and again, the entire village would move to a different location. There, the new land would be cleared and burned as before, and good harvests could again be obtained. Excavations of Neolithic farming villages in China have revealed that sites were repeatedly abandoned and reoccupied by the same tribes. This is not surprising, as land that has been exhausted by overcultivation will regain its fertility after lying fallow for several years, and by returning to a previously occupied site, farmers were able to reuse house foundations, saving labor.

Pottery found at Banpo, a Neolithic archaeological site on the outskirts of Xi'an. The farming village is believed to have been inhabited from approximately 4500 B.C. to 3750 B.C. China's civilization emerged from farming communities such as this one.

In the vast plains north of the Yellow River, farming was difficult because rainfall was not reliable and the strong winds blowing across the prairie damaged young crops. The grassy plains, though, were perfect for raising herd animals. The hunters in that region learned to domesticate wild horses and cattle. They supplemented their diet of wild game with meat and milk from their herds. Eventually these herders learned to ride their horses, which gave a new speed and power to their hunting and migration patterns.

Conflicting Ways of Life

The natural conflict between herders and farmers would prove to be a recurring and intractable issue in Chinese life for thousands of years. Though they moved periodically, Neolithic farmers built semi-permanent settlements, even fencing off sections of their villages for raising pigs and firing pottery in communal kilns. Farmers protected their villages from wild animals and floods with either dirt

The Chinese Creation Story

The Chinese creation story seems to have originated with the Miao cultures of the south. Although variations of the story have been discovered, the version that became the established legend in the overall Chinese culture is as follows.

In the beginning, there was a cosmic egg filled with chaos. Pan Ku was born inside the egg. One day he took a hammer and chisel and chopped the shell in two. The top part became the bright heavens; the bottom part became the murky, heavy earth. For 18,000 years, Pan Ku held the bright sky up over the earth. He grew 10 feet a year during this time, until the sky was so far up that it could never fall into the earth. Finally, Pan Ku died. His giant body transformed into various natural forces and objects. For example, his bones became the mountains, and his bone marrow became pearls and jade. The rivers were formed from his blood, and the rains from his perspiration. The wind came from his breath. One of his eyes became the sun, and the other the moon. Trees and grasses sprang from his hair.

In the primary myth, the insects that fed on the giant's corpse became humankind. In a secondary myth, the goddess Nu Wa was told to make people. She started to model persons out of yellow clay, but the job was so big she got tired. So she took her belt and dipped it into the mud. The mud specks that dropped off became the rest of humankind. The few people that she had made from the yellow clay were the rich nobles and rulers. The many people arising from the mud droplets were the mass of commoners. Thus the idea of separate classes was established very early in Chinese thinking, and this idea of stratified society prevailed for thousands of years.

walls or ditches. Growing fields lay outside the village. The larger and more reliable food supply that agriculture made possible, combined with the relatively safe lifestyle of farming, led to a steady increase in the farmer population. Feeding the continually expanding population, in turn, required more and more land.

In comparison with the lifestyle of farmers, Neolithic herders had a harsh existence. They lived in animal-hide tents and had to move almost constantly in search of fresh forage for their herds. The rigors of the nomadic lifestyle ensured that, while the population of herders might increase gradually, it would never match the explosive growth of the farming population.

It is not difficult to imagine the trouble that occurred when herders and farmers came into contact with each other—when, for example, a group of horsemen and their animals happened upon a field of young millet shoots. As farmers cultivated more and more of the land to feed their growing population, such encounters would have become more frequent, creating the need for protection against the increasingly fierce horsemen. A specialized ruling and military class thus arose. Even as far back as Neolithic times, the farming peoples of China tried to push the nomadic herding tribes north of the increasingly prosperous farms along the Yellow River. The Chinese culture to come would include awareness of a constant threat from the north.

Evidence of Growing Social and Cultural Complexity

In the south, with its monsoon climate, root crops such as taro and yams were cultivated first. Wet-cultivated rice began to be grown around 4500 B.C. This type of cultivation is fairly complicated. First, protected seed beds are planted with rice seeds. When the sprouts are eight or nine inches high, fields need to be plowed, heavily fertilized with organic matter, and then flooded to a depth

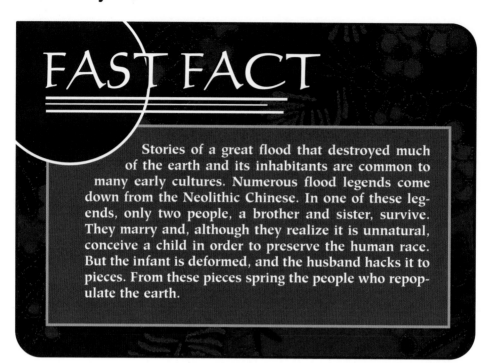

FAST FACT

Stories of a great flood that destroyed much of the earth and its inhabitants are common to many early cultures. Numerous flood legends come down from the Neolithic Chinese. In one of these legends, only two people, a brother and sister, survive. They marry and, although they realize it is unnatural, conceive a child in order to preserve the human race. But the infant is deformed, and the husband hacks it to pieces. From these pieces spring the people who repopulate the earth.

of about eight inches. The seedlings are transplanted by hand into the flooded field, and the field must stay flooded throughout the entire growing season. When the rice is mature, the field has to be drained so that the grain can be harvested.

The cultivation of rice provides clues about the growing complexity of Neolithic society in China. The rice farmers had to devise, build, and maintain effective irrigation. This would have required not only a fairly high degree of technical sophistication but also a good deal of coordinated labor. Many people would also have had to work together in planting the seedlings, draining the fields, and harvesting the rice. All this shows that a relatively complex social organization had developed.

Neolithic people had also begun to think about abstract ideas, including the question of what happens to a person after death. The positioning of bodies and the presence of grave goods in Neolithic burials show that special rites were followed at death. Moreover, the inclusion of valuable and useful items with the deceased is evidence of the belief in an afterlife (where the dead would need the supplies that were interred with the body). The Chinese culture later expanded this basic idea into a poetic, three-stage cycle of life: before birth, the "seasons" of life, and the ultimate transfer to the spirit world.

Jade artifacts occasionally found in Neolithic graves are particularly interesting because the mineral nephrite (jade) is not found in China but occurs in Siberia and in the Middle East. Is it possible there were active trade routes to these regions 6,000 or 7,000 years ago? Even more perplexing is the question of how these objects were worked. Jade is so hard that it cannot be cut or chipped like softer stone; it cannot even be carved by metal. The only way to work jade is with grinding and drilling actions. In Han times several thousand years later, abrasives were added to the grinding process to speed up progress. Even so, without modern laser technology and supersonic drills, jade carving is a slow, laborious process. The skilled ancient craftspersons who ground and polished jade must have been fed and housed by other members of Neolithic communities. This shows increasing task specialization in society. Since small jade amulets and tools have been found in some Neolithic graves, one might surmise that jade was already revered as a nearly indestructible material, a fitting valuable to accompany the spirits into the eternal "invisible world" after death.

Archaeologists have found evidence of many other inventions made by Neolithic tribes in China. Among them are the potter's wheel, silk and hemp woven fabrics, and the beginnings of writing (139 single word "signs" have been catalogued so far). Around the same time as these advances were occurring in China, other Neolithic cultures were flourishing in Sumeria, between the Tigris and Euphrates Rivers in present-day Iraq, and in Egypt. Important patterns for human society were laid down during Neolithic times. In China, these patterns would become the Chinese Way.

Oracle bones, used to foretell the future, began to appear toward the end of the Xia dynasty (ca. 2000 B.C.–ca. 1600 B.C.) but were especially favored by the rulers of the Shang dynasty (ca. 1700 B.C.–ca. 1027 B.C.). The characters engraved on this oracle bone are the earliest known examples of Chinese pictograph writing.

3

The Legendary Emperors and the Xia Dynasty

The Neolithic period saw dramatic innovations that enabled society to develop and thrive. In China most of the credit for these advances is given to a single semi-mythical figure: Huang Di, who is said to have lived around 2700 to 2600 B.C. The first of China's legendary Five Emperors, Huang Di is traditionally considered the founder of Chinese civilization and is said to have invented (or encouraged his subjects to invent) writing, the pottery wheel, medicine, the first calendar, and the magnetic compass, among numerous other fundamental advances. Huang Di's wife is credited with the domestication of silkworms and the development of fabric clothing. Legend says that his reign saw the invention of the wheel and armor, as well as the "South Pointing Chariot"—an amazing creation of interlocking gears topped by a figure that always points in the same direction, regardless of which way the chariot is turned. Stories tell how this creation enabled Huang Di—known as the Yellow Emperor—to lead his army out of a dense fog and win victory in a decisive battle (though the South Pointing Chariot may actually have been invented around 400 B.C., during the Warring States period).

In the social realm, Huang Di supposedly brought order by assigning the family name to the separate clans and each of their family members (this highlights the great importance Chinese culture placed on family identity from the very beginning). The Yellow Emperor is also said to have originated many ceremonies, including sacrifices.

Clearly, Huang Di is the embodiment of 5,000-odd years of Neolithic progress in China. Nevertheless, the legendary Yellow Emperor was probably based in part on a historical ruler, possibly a leader of the Yangshao culture, which flourished from about 5000 B.C. to about 3000 B.C. The yellow of the emperor's title reflects the Nu Wa legend—in which the nobles were molded out of yellow clay. In later Chinese civilization, only the emperor could wear the mustard-yellow color called "imperial yellow." Yellow symbolizing earth and a color reserved for the emperor carried through to Chinese culture for thousands of years.

Successors to the Yellow Emperor

After the reign of Huang Di, rule eventually went to his 16-year-old great-great-grandson Yao, the fourth of China's legendary Five Emperors. Yao was a kind ruler, and his reign started off well. But disaster struck one day as 10 suns appeared (some scientists have suggested that this story describes a meteor impact), creating huge fires and making the rivers boil. Fierce animals fled from the burning forests and attacked the people. Yao asked the archer Prince Yi to help. Yi shot and killed 9 of the suns, but Yao stopped him from killing the 10th, as he knew the people needed a sun.

Toward the end of his life, Yao set about looking for a successor. He did not want his own son, who was cruel and treacherous, to rule because he feared that harm might befall the people.

Eventually Yao heard of a man named Shun, who had been born to parents of bad character but who had managed to change them for the better by living according to moral principles. Yao gave two of his daughters to Shun as wives and brought him to the capital. For three years Yao assigned Shun difficult tasks to test his abilities. Shun accomplished each task without complaint, and Yao asked him to be co-emperor. After a period of joint rule, Yao abdicated, leaving Shun as the sole emperor.

Shun, the last of the legendary Five Emperors, proved as capable as his predecessors had been. He was confronted with a difficult, recurring problem: the flooding of the Yellow River. His chief engineer, Gun, tried to solve the problem by building dikes to keep the river in its banks. But the floods were so strong that the dikes kept breaking, creating even worse devastation. The engineer's son, Yu, thought a new approach should be taken, but Gun stubbornly insisted on rebuilding the dikes.

Emperor Shun decided to elevate Yu to the position of chief engineer and assigned the flood problem to him. Instead of trying to build up higher dikes, Yu dug down to make the river's channel deeper. He also created spill channels where floodwater could collect and run off to the sea without damaging fields and villages. After more than a decade of hard work, the flood problem was under control.

A grateful Shun persuaded the clan leaders to ratify Yu as his co-ruler. Upon Shun's death, Yu tried to step aside, in order to permit Shun's son to take the throne. But the people clamored for Yu instead, and while succession generally was determined by birthright, it was customary for clan leaders to give their approval to the claim of a new king. Faced with a choice between the accomplished Yu and a candidate whose only qualification was birthright, they picked the former, and Yu ascended the throne.

Yu went on to found the Xia dynasty, which is thought by some, but not all, to be China's first true dynasty. Before his time, kings were ratified by general acclaim of the clan leaders. Yu, it is said, established that the right to rule would be strictly hereditary.

The Xia: China's First Bronze Age Culture

With the exception of Yu, the legendary heroes of early China originated in the late Neolithic Longshan culture of the Yellow River valley. Because this culture was pre-literate—and its stories were passed down orally for many generations before finally being recorded, centuries after the events they supposedly describe—separating the historical from the mythical can be difficult. Much is known about the shape of Neolithic society from the archaeological record—from the settlements, burial sites, tools, pottery, and other objects left behind—but without written records, drawing conclusions about specific events or rulers is largely a matter of speculation.

An artistic rendering of Emperor Yu, founder of the Xia dynasty.

The legendary Five Emperors of ancient China are Huang Di, Juan Xu, Gu, Yao, and Shun, who is said to have reigned just before the founding of the Xia dynasty by Emperor Yu.

The Neolithic period, the last part of the Stone Age, was followed by the Bronze Age. During this time, people learned how to smelt copper and tin to create the alloy bronze. The metal was used to fashion stronger and better tools and weapons than could be made from stone, which helped spur a variety of cultural changes.

Until recently, many archaeologists believed that the Shang dynasty, which arose around 1600 B.C., was the first Bronze Age culture in China. Shang bronze ritual items, even those fashioned in the culture's early period, are exquisitely formed and indicate advanced technology. The early Shang also had a clear and sophisticated system of writing, as evidenced by the oracle bones upon which they wrote questions for (and answers from) the gods.

In the view of certain archaeologists, however, something didn't seem quite right with the standard view of the Shang as China's first Bronze Age culture. How could advanced metal technology and fully formed writing spring forth so suddenly? The answer offered by historians was that the Chinese had learned metal making and writing from contact with Middle Eastern civilizations. Yet such a theory seemed at odds with the work of the great Chinese historian Sima Qian. After ascending to the post of grand historian for the Han court in 107 B.C., Sima Qian collected all the old

This *jue*, or wine vessel, is an example of Xia bronze work. Once thought to be entirely mythical, the Xia are now widely regarded as China's first Bronze Age culture.

writings that had escaped a nationwide book burning a century earlier. He used these sources in creating the *Shiji* (*Records of the Grand Historian*), the first comprehensive written history of China. In this 130-chapter work, considered a masterpiece of historical writing, the legendary Five Emperors sound like fantastical myths, but Yu and the later Xia emperors come across as real people. According to Sima Qian, the Xia could write, and they also made metal weapons and ritual items.

Partly on the basis of Sima Qian's history, some modern scholars believed that the Xia dynasty had existed, even though many others insisted that the stories about the dynasty were purely mythical. Those who espoused the former view hoped that archaeology would one day prove the case. In the end, this is precisely what happened.

By the 1990s archaeologists excavating at Erlitou, a Neolithic site in central China that had first been discovered in 1959, began to recognize different layers at the site as the remains of three successive cultures: the Yangshao, Longshan, and Xia. Erlitou had been a capital of the last of these cultures, the Xia, which flourished from around 2000 B.C. to around 1600 B.C. From the evidence uncovered—first primarily at Erlitou but later at various sites, especially in Henan Province—archaeologists concluded that the Xia had learned to make bronze independently of, and a bit earlier than, Middle Eastern cultures. The Xia had also developed pictogram writing.

The Xia capital near present-day Yangcheng (Sima Qian identified six Xia capitals) covered 55 acres. A palace area was built on a tamped-earth platform; similar platforms are seen with all imperial Chinese palaces for the next 4,000 years. A separate section of the capital contained workshops for bronze making and crafts.

The basic unit of the Xia kingdom was the walled town or village. Several walled towns together made up a vassal state. Each vassal state was headed by a clan leader, who owed allegiance to the king. The rise of this hierarchical political structure accompanied important changes in agriculture. The slash-and-burn system of

The Xia dynasty controlled a relatively small area north of the Yellow River.

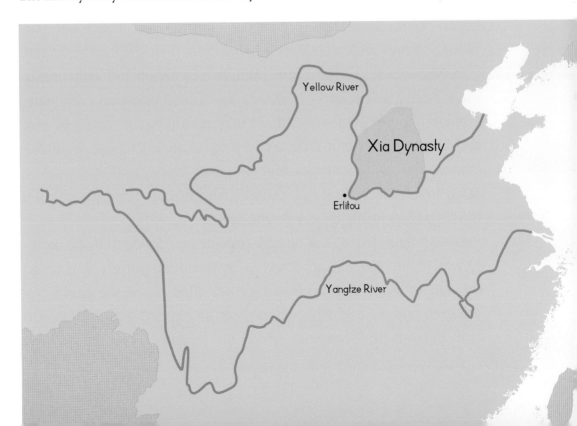

Neolithic farming, by which agricultural communities periodically moved, had been replaced by a system that allowed for permanent farming villages. Under the new system, farming villages let some of their fields lie fallow on a rotating basis, which prevented the soil's fertility from being exhausted. This approach required clearly defined, stable land boundaries, which in turn necessitated centralized control and military protection.

Evidence for increasing stratification in Xia society is found in the culture's bronzes. The archaeological record indicates that bronze items—ritual vessels, knives, and weapons—were made only for the ruling class; the agricultural tools of commoners continued to be fashioned from stone and wood. The Xia bronze wares that have been discovered are well made. They have simple surfaces and are fashioned in shapes that would prevail for the next thousand years. A variety of Xia bronze weapons have been found. A pointed, hammer-like bronze head was attached to a wooden pole to create a deadly implement believed to have been swung by soldiers fighting from "war wagons." Many large, heart-shaped bronze spear points have been uncovered. In hand-to-hand combat, bronze swords were used.

In Xia society, warfare and military protection are believed to have been the exclusive province of nobles and their retainers; common people evidently did not take part in battles (evidence for this comes from Sima Qian as well as various Chinese legends). Princes and their warriors met on open fields, and Xia warfare often involved elements of chivalry and honor. The princes rode horses and possibly used war chariots.

As with its bronzes, Xia pottery provides evidence that the society was highly specialized. Previously, Neolithic pottery had relied on coils of rolled clay pressed together; almost anyone could create such pottery, and without much of an expenditure of time. Xia craftspersons, by contrast, used the recently invented potter's wheel to shape incredibly thin-walled black bowls and beakers. Museum curators call the Xia high-fired black ceramics "eggshell ware" because the walls are less than 1/16 of an inch, or a single millimeter, thick. Acquiring the skill to fashion such pieces would have required considerable time, and clearly these artisans were not farmers making pottery in their spare moments.

The Xia also used oracle bones—which would be a feature of Chinese culture for the next thousand years. It is believed that simple Neolithic fertility rites were supplemented with the beginnings of ancestor worship, and the rituals were an important function of the ruling class. Because the older Neolithic cultures and the future Shang offered human sacrifices to the gods, it is assumed that the Xia rulers did so as well, but thus far no direct evidence of this has been found.

The Xia dynasty lasted through the reigns of 17 rulers. The first, Yu, was an admirable administrator and competent strategist. His immediate successors were said to be lazy and pleasure seeking. At one point, the palace minister Hanzhou took advantage of the weakness and usurped the throne, killing off the imperial family. The traditional tale recounts that Empress Xiang, who was pregnant, was able to escape to her own clan for protection and gave birth to a boy named Shaoking, who was raised with the ambition to someday recover the throne. He managed to do this, and he and his immediate successors were apparently good rulers. Eventually, however, the Xia rulers seem to have become increasingly tyrannical. Graves in the villages show greater numbers of

This high-stemmed drinking cup is an example of the black "eggshell ware" pottery created by highly skilled Xia craftspersons.

Yu, Founder of the Xia Dynasty

Yu is said to have had a magical birth. It is even claimed that he was the son of a god. According to the traditional account of his life, Yu was made prince of the state of Xia as a young man. He had just gotten married when he was called by Emperor Shun to fix the flood problem. So Yu left his new wife and went to the capital.

Yu was a methodical thinker. He first went to the flood site himself, where he saw the broken dikes. There he made observations on his own and consulted the workers directly. He noticed that water flowed naturally from high to low places, and he decided to take advantage of this fact. Instead of having the workers build up, he ordered them to dig down, making the river deeper and deeper the nearer to the sea they got. He even had side channels dug, to make the river run even faster to the sea.

Yu, it is said, worked right alongside the workers, digging and hauling earth away. He was so dedicated that it was said that he three times refrained from

trauma injuries, indicating that more and more strife occurred as time went on. The last of the Xia kings, Jie, is considered one of China's worst tyrants. According to the traditional retelling of events, his weakness for beautiful women would play a major role in his undoing, and in the demise of the Xia dynasty. Jie launched a military expedition against a neighboring state and was given a beautiful girl as a gift to convince him to withdraw. Jie began to spend all his time with this new concubine, and he conscripted many farmers to build her a luxurious palace. His subjects hated his extravagance and tyranny, and many no longer felt bound to

entering the door of his home when he was passing by, saying, "I don't have a family until the flood is under control."

After 13 hard years, the river had been dredged and the canals dug, and the flooding was under control. Farmers who had fled to the high mountains could now return to their farms. Life returned to peaceful prosperity. The people started to call the engineer "Yu the Great." Emperor Shun was so impressed with Yu's competence and dedication that he recommended the clans select Yu as his co-ruler.

After Shun's death, Yu became the emperor. Because he was also a prince of Xia, his name was Xia Yu. This is how his dynasty was named Xia.

Emperor Yu toured the nine vassal states of his realm. He had nine large, three-legged metal cauldrons known as *dings* created to represent each state. These objects were passed down from emperor to emperor as symbols of imperial rule, until they were lost in the Warring States period 1,500 years after Yu's death.

serve him. The kingdom was ripe for change, which was to come in the form of a fierce conqueror from the east, the Shang.

Despite all these problems, later Chinese would regard the Xia dynasty as a golden age. The question is, why? Chinese sages looked back on the stability of the town structure, when vassal princes protected their clan's farmers from marauding raiders, with nostalgia for the fresh beginnings of their civilization. They admired the benevolent kings, who performed the rituals and ceremonies to the ancestors and the gods. The memory of the imagined Xia golden age would be an enduring feature in Chinese culture.

A bronze *ding*, or tripod, from the Shang dynasty. The top part of the vessel features a *taotie*, or monster-like mask, which was a common decorative element during this period. The *taotie* is thought to be a clan crest.

4

Shang Dynasty: War and Grandeur

Violence raged during the twilight of the Xia dynasty. Clans fought one another for territory and slaves, and the tyrannical and decadent last Xia king, Jie, no longer commanded the power to prevent this fighting. Warfare had traditionally been an activity reserved for the nobility, but Cheng Tang, tribal chieftain of the Tzu clan from the Shandong Peninsula, armed the peasants. After many years of fighting, his forces finally defeated the Xia king in central China. Subsequently, peasant rebellions would become a common feature of dynastic overthrows in China into the 20th century.

Around 1766 B.C. Cheng Tang was awarded the imperial seals and Emperor Yu's nine bronze tripods (*dings*), the symbols of Xia rule. Cheng Tang founded the Shang dynasty—considered the first great Chinese state—which ruled for 700 years before its overthrow around 1045 B.C. At its height the Shang state covered a large area north and south of the Yellow River, from the Shandong Peninsula in the east to the Loess Plateau in the west. Although the first capital was at Bo, in today's Shandong Province, the capital was later moved south and west to Yin, near today's Anyang in Henan Province. This is where archaeologists have made the richest finds from the Shang era.

The Shang were warlike, energetic, practical, and thorough. Expanding on the foundations laid down by the Xia, they developed a vital, vibrantly effective culture. Whereas the Xia had lived in towns and villages, the Shang appear to have been the first Chinese people to develop large cities complete with

The fearsome Shang emerged from the Shandong Peninsula to overthrow the Xia dynasty and establish control over a much larger area. The Shang dynasty eventually moved its capital to Yin.

temples, palaces, workshops, and military encampments. Court life was a glittering round of state rituals, preparations for war, strategy sessions, consultations with the gods, acceptance of tribute gifts from other clans, and noble births, illnesses, deaths, and funerals.

Foundations of Shang Rule

Shang power rested on physical as well as spiritual foundations, and for the Tzu ruling class, bronze played a key role in both aspects. The Tzu were able to maintain a monopoly on bronze

One reason the Shang were able to hold power was their monopoly over the making of bronze weapons and ritual instruments. Shown here is the head of an ornamented bronze *yue*, an ancient Chinese weapon similar to an axe, on display at the Shanghai Museum.

making because they were the only ones wealthy and powerful enough to muster the enormous resources that the process required: huge amounts of metal ore, wood fuel, and human labor. And bronze, in turn, gave the Shang rulers a decisive military advantage, as wood and stone weapons are no match for metal ones. Riding into battle in fearsome bronze-wheeled chariots, and armed with bronze weapons such as battle-axes and spears, Shang warriors easily conquered the less technologically developed tribes. Within the Shang realm, the nobility's monopoly on bronze weapons was a powerful deterrent to rebellion.

If their bronze monopoly gave the Shang unrivaled might on the battlefield, it also helped guarantee their rule in a less obvious way—by lending the dynasty legitimacy. Cheng Tang, the founder of the dynasty, had derived much of his power from a Xia people grateful to be rid of their oppressive ruler. Subsequent Shang kings could not count on this goodwill. They developed a complex rationale for rule that was based on the unique status they claimed in spiritual matters, and bronze played a key role in the rituals designed to maintain this status.

The legitimacy of Shang rule came from their exclusive connection with the gods. Shang Di—the Shang High Lord, or the Lord on High—was said to be the founding ancestor of the Shang Tzu clan. Of course, he was accessible only to the Shang Tzu ruler and to the ruler's ancestors. It was believed that Shang Di and the king's ancestors actively ruled the natural realm—the king was merely their living representative on earth. When a king died, he would join the Shang ancestors and thus continue to influence human events.

The ruling Tzu clan employed shamans to communicate with their powerful ancestors. Animal spirits were the messengers. Questions were asked of the ancestor gods, and the patterns of cracks that appeared on prepared animal bones to which heat was applied were interpreted for the answers. Animal sacrifices were performed to please the ancestors. Wine was heated and offered to them. The imposing, heavy bronze ritual vessels, designed in the same shapes as the clay pots and vessels common people used to cook and serve their own food, were the cooking and serving vessels the Tzu rulers used to ritually feed their powerful Shang ancestor gods. Huge gong-like bells were struck to alert the gods when a ritual was about to begin. Increasingly complex and imposing public rituals created a sense of awe in the people ruled by the Shang. Only the rulers could make and use bronze, and without bronze, the rulers' ancestor gods, who influenced events on earth, could not be propitiated and asked to rule justly. Without the elaborate bronze ritual vessels, the ancestor gods would not reveal what the future would bring when the shamans cracked the animal messenger bones.

Thus the monopoly on bronze was used to ensure Shang power. That is why the only bronze objects found at Shang sites are weapons and ritual vessels. Bronze agricultural implements would have improved farming technology—and hence the lives of peasants—immeasurably.

The Shang, like other ancient Chinese cultures, are known to have conducted human sacrifices. These remains of sacrificial victims were uncovered at a Shang site near Zhengzhou in Henan Province.

Some art connoisseurs credit the Shang with the finest bronze pieces ever created. This detail, from a Shang bronze ritual vessel, depicts the face of an owl.

But that is not something the Shang rulers were interested in, and it would be a thousand years before metal tools were created for use in agriculture and ordinary home life.

Social Structure

Shang society was divided into four classes: the ruling family of the Tzu clan; the other members of the noble Tzu clan, who served as feudal lords and state officials; the common people; and slaves. The nobles were educated and lived in palaces in the well-organized cities. The commoners farmed the nobles' lands or worked in crafts. Slaves did the same work as commoners but could also be used as human sacrifices.

Chinese people through the ages have referred to the Shang era as the Slave Society. This does not mean that most people were slaves—only criminals, prisoners of war, and children of slaves were officially slaves. However, later Chinese realized that the more numerous "free" commoners were little more than slaves. At any time they could be conscripted for military service or compelled to work as laborers on state projects, and when not so engaged they were totally at the mercy of the nobles whose lands they tilled or workshops they toiled in.

Although society was organized along patriarchal lines, with each family headed by the oldest male, the Shang valued ability and results above gender—at least among the nobility. Women in the noble classes were educated and could go as far as their talents for war or government took them. In fact, Fu Hao (Lady Hao), the third wife of King Wu Ding, was a great general who personally led armies on vast military campaigns. Archaeologists have found numerous oracle bones asking about the outcomes of her impending battles, as well as several oracle bones from different dates asking whether her baby would be male or female.

Family structure was complex and, perhaps not surprisingly, varied according to social position. Noble males frequently had several wives at the same time, in addition to many concubines, who were essentially lesser wives. A major reason for this was to ensure plenty of male children in the ruling family, so that the dynasty would not die out (a major fear during a time when many people died young). When a king died, rule went first to his brothers (from oldest to youngest). In some regions, when a man died young, his wife automatically married his next younger brother. Some translations of the ancient scripts appear to show that in the poorer classes, several males (probably brothers) sometimes supported and shared a single wife.

The Shang believed that after death, the ruler and ruling nobles traveled to the invisible world of the royal ancestors, from where they continued to affect earthly events. Hence it was important to equip the departed with everything necessary to continue their activities and to enjoy the afterlife. This is why excavations of Shang royal tombs have yielded so many artifacts—and in the process shed much light on the culture. Bronze ritual vessels, gong-bells, food, oracle bone records, clothes, jewelry, weapons, and other treasured implements were interred in the royal tombs. Entire war chariots with horses were sometimes even buried. And human attendants and entertainers—probably slaves who had been sacrificed—accompanied deceased nobles on the journey to the afterlife as well.

Technological and Cultural Advances

The Shang dynasty is the first Chinese civilization that left extensive written records. Most of the writing is found on oracle bones and bronze ritual vessels. Large rocks were sometimes inscribed with details about important state events. Early Chinese historians noted that the Shang also wrote on strips of bamboo. Whereas in ancient Egypt and Mesopotamia, the first writing was used for commercial records (grain measures and taxes), the writing found at Shang sites consists of religious divinations—questions for the ancestor gods, and the gods' answers.

The following are some of the oracle bone inscriptions found in Lady Hao's tomb:

Shall Fu Hao have a fortunate birth [that is, a boy]? The king prognosticated, saying, "If she gives birth on a jia day there will be misfortune."

Shall Fu Hao have a fortunate birth? The king prognosticated, saying, "If she gives birth on a ding day it shall be fortunate; if on a geng day, it shall be greatly auspicious." On the thirty-third day thereafter, on jia-yin, Fu Hao gave birth. It was not fortunate; it was a girl.

Should Fu Hao follow Guo of Zhi and attack the [name undecipherable] tribe, with the king attacking Zhonglu from the east toward the place where Fu Hao shall be?

This piece of bone is inscribed with ancient Chinese pictographs that describe a royal tiger hunt. Nobles in China hunted for food as well as sport.

If the king does not order Fu Hao to follow Guo of Zhi and attack the [*name undecipherable*] tribe, will we not perhaps receive support?

Fu Hao is ill; is there some evil influence?

Should we perform a sacrifice to Father Yi on behalf of Fu Hao, and sacrifice a lamb, decapitate a boar, and sacrifice ten sets of sheep and pig?

In the artistic realm, the Shang dynasty's highest accomplishment is its astonishing bronze ritual vessels, which some art connoisseurs consider the finest bronzes ever created. The Shang perfected the technique of piece molding with clay master forms, so several identical vessels or bells could be created from the same mold. In large outdoor bronze factories, the laborers used an early assembly line manufacturing process to make and finish these fabulous objects. Ornamentation was bold and usually involved realistic or mythical animal forms. The animal-based *taotie* "monster mask" was a central feature of all the ritual objects. Because this motif is first seen with the Shang and disappeared after they were overthrown, it is believed that this horned animal design was a Tzu clan crest of some sort. The sense of bold design and skillful craftsmanship of Shang bronze works has never been surpassed. It is certainly fitting that later Chinese characterized the Shang dynasty with the color white, representing the element metal.

The Shang made major advances in town planning and the organization of large populations. They first established the city-within-a-city configuration for government centers. The inner city, which was enclosed by walls, contained the palace and seat of government; the outer city consisted of trading centers, homes, and workshops. These palace cities were carefully laid out, with special

Lady Hao: Military General, Royal Wife, and Mother

The infant girl who was to become Lady Hao was born to the chieftain of an important tribe of hunting and trading nomads to the north of Shang territory. As a girl, she was quick to learn and showed special skill in horsemanship and falconry (hunting for small game with trained birds of prey).

Around 1200 B.C., Hao's father learned that the Shang king Wu Ding was planning to attack his tribe in a campaign to expand Shang borders. Rather than risk an almost certain defeat at the hands of the fearsome Shang army—which would result in the enslavement of his people—Hao's father negotiated to join the Shang as a subject state. As a sign of his goodwill, he sent his daughter Hao as a wife to Wu Ding, along with many gifts and valuable warhorses. That is how the young Hao became Lady Hao, the third wife of King Wu Ding.

Wu Ding soon found that, in addition to her outstanding horsemanship, his new wife possessed a grasp of strategy equal to that of any of his generals. She rode with the king on his military campaigns. In performing sacrifices and rituals she was imposing, and in managing her assigned state projects she was

walkways officials could use to make sure that everything was in order. The site at Anyang shows evidence of drainage ditch systems, possibly running under the major buildings. K. C. Chang, in his book *Early Chinese Civilization: Anthropological Perspectives*, writes that the ancestral temple, the imposing site where the rituals and divinations took place, was the first public building erected in

decisive and fair. Courtiers and common people alike came to respect and love Lady Hao. The king made her an honorary Shang Tzu clan member and ordered that new objects made for her include the *taotie* symbol.

The military especially held Hao in high regard. Finally, the king awarded her a special bronze axe with her name inscribed on it. This was a general's axe, and it gave her the authority to lead the king's troops. She is known to have commanded an army of 13,000 soldiers in a victory against the Guifang, tribes of "barbarians" who had invaded Shang territory.

Lady Hao had several children, all girls. She died young, from an illness, and was mourned by all. Since the king was still living, Lady Hao could not be buried in his tomb. Instead, a special tomb was built for her in the royal cemetery with a small memorial hall over it. As was the practice, in addition to the grave treasures for her use in the afterlife, 16 men, women, and children were sacrificed and buried with Hao to serve her. Six dogs were also buried in the tomb. Over her body was laid her general's axe, a small stone sculpture of a falcon from her days as a nomad princess, and a small jade phoenix bird from Neolithic times.

a new city. Next came the treasury, the palace, and the military barracks. Finally, outside the walls of the inner city, the markets, workshops, and homes for the common people were constructed.

Under the Shang, homes for the common people remained essentially the same as the houses of Neolithic villagers—round pit homes with straw roofs. But in the design of public buildings and

FAST FACT

The tomb of Fu Hao—containing some 2,000 exquisite grave objects, many identified with her name—was discovered in Anyang in 1976. Although not overly grand by the standards of Chinese royal tombs, it had escaped grave robbers. Thus its significance is comparable to that of the tomb of Tutankhamen in Egypt, which had also lain untouched for thousands of years and provided archaeologists with a treasure trove of information. Lady Hao's tomb has been restored in the Yin Ruins Garden-Museum of Anyang and is a popular tourist site.

palaces, the Shang established the key architectural elements that would prevail in China for the next 3,500 years. These structures were designed as large rectangles set on raised earth or stone platforms. Wood columns supported roof rafters (in Shang times the roofs of public buildings, like those of the pit homes, were made of thatched straw). The walls were filled in with tamped earth, but they were not load bearing—the thick walls simply kept the weather out and gave security to the inhabitants. The overall effect was simple but imposing.

Although the use of bronze tools could have greatly advanced agriculture, as noted, metal was reserved for war and ritual. Even so, agriculture and food production progressed during Shang times. In addition to the horses used for war and hunting, other animals were domesticated, including cows, oxen, pigs, dogs, chickens, and ducks. Meat from domesticated animals was supplemented with wild game. The nobles hunted to keep up their military skills as well as to provide meat for the royal table. In fact, the Shang diet for the nobility consisted largely of meat. Alcohol was also available to the elite, but generally wine was reserved for religious rituals. The biggest agricultural breakthrough in Shang times was the discovery of the soybean. Not only is this bean resistant to drought, but it is also high in protein. Soybeans, the main component of tofu, have been a staple of Chinese meals ever since.

To facilitate trade, the Shang developed the concept of money (cowry shells functioned as the currency). Lady Hao's tomb contained more than 6,900 of these shells, a fortune for her to spend in the afterlife.

Despite all these advances, the essential character of Shang civilization remained uncompromising force. In such a culture, whose elites had little concern for the plight of ordinary people, the risk that cruelty would evolve from the habit of force was always present. In fact, the last Shang king, Di Xin, and his wife were infamous for their delight in devising ever more excruciating and unusual tortures. The misery of the people led to widespread discontent, and the fierceness of the Shang ways became too extreme for acceptance as a basis for ongoing Chinese civilization. In the end, the dynasty was overthrown around 1045 B.C. by the more tolerant Zhou clan.

A bronze incense-burner from the Zhou era. After the Zhou overthrew the Shang, they added new gods and goddesses to the Chinese pantheon and created new rituals.

Western Zhou: An Age of Peace and Prosperity

The overthrow of the Shang dynasty was remarkably similar to the downfall of the earlier Xia dynasty. Both dynasties began with good rulers but ended with cruel and debauched tyrants. The Shang came out of the east to overthrow the Xia. The Zhou came from the west to topple the Shang.

Di Xin, the last Shang ruler, alienated the people by his extreme cruelty and by squandering the country's riches. Moreover, he lost the support of many of the nobles by punishing any who counseled him to change his ways. But there was also a religious basis for the end of Shang rule. The British China scholar Herbert Allen Giles (1845–1935) emphasized this dimension in chronicling the dynasty's demise:

When the Shang dynasty sank into the lowest depths of moral abasement, King Wu [of the Zhou clan], who charged himself with its overthrow, and who subsequently became the first sovereign of the [Zhou] dynasty, offered sacrifices to Almighty God [Shang Di], and also to Mother Earth. "The King of Shang," he said in his address to the high officers who collected around him, "does not revere God above, and inflicts calamities on the people below. Almighty God is moved with indignation." On the day of the final battle he declared that he was acting in the matter of punishment merely as the instrument of God; and after his great victory and the establishment of his own line, it was to God [Shang Di] that he rendered thanks.

In the decisive battle at Mu-ye near Anyang, the Shang tyrant Di Xin ordered his army to attack, but the soldiers refused and turned their spears to the sky. Seeing this, Di Xin committed suicide. King Wu of the Zhou tribe was awarded the seals of rule and the nine bronze tripods (*dings*) from the ancient emperor Yu. This marked the beginning of the Zhou dynasty.

Revising Belief Systems and the Mandate to Rule

For almost 700 years the Zhou tribe had been ruled by the Shang. After all this time, the Zhou shared the same language and culture as the Shang. More important, they shared the same religion. Shang Di, the founding ancestor of the Shang Tzu clan, was everyone's High Lord. So the Zhou had a problem: wouldn't the Shang High Lord be angry that the Zhou tribe had just overthrown Shang Di's descendants?

The Zhou priests and ministers solved this problem in several ways. They gradually made Shang Di more abstract. The Zhou priests taught that Shang Di was the Lord of the High Heavens,

In the Zhou dynasty, use of bells took on greater significance in religious observances. Pictured here are a collection of bronze striking bells and a detail from a wine container showing bell players.

somewhere far away and inaccessible to everyone. They de-emphasized the original concept that Shang Di was the founding ancestor of the Shang Tzu clan. Other gods became as important as the Shang ancestor gods—the Queen Mother of the West, the water god, the sky god, and so forth. The Zhou performed fewer divinations with oracle bones than had the Shang, and the importance of animals and shamans as messengers to the ancestors declined. In the revised Zhou rituals, bells took on more importance; their sounds became prayer messengers to the gods. Bells throughout the Zhou kingdom were tuned to the exact pitch as the king's bells, so the entire nation could use the same booming tones at once to summon the gods.

The most important rationale for Zhou rule was the concept of the Mandate of Heaven. In Shang times it was generally accepted that the gods would send trouble if they were displeased with the actions of the earthly ruler. The Zhou took this concept one step further, proposing that the gods would actually withdraw the right to rule from an unworthy king and award it to a more virtuous individual. This idea of human virtue and merit is known as *Te*.

"In the earlier period," K. C. Chang suggests in his book *Early Chinese Civilization: Anthropological Perspectives,* "the mythological animal served as a link between the world of man and the world of the ancestors and the gods, and . . . in later periods when the world of the ancestors and the gods were forcibly separated, the animal was identified with the world of the gods and became a symbol against which men struggled as though they were struggling against the gods." Chang thus points out evidence in Zhou beliefs of increasing humanism—that is to say, more reliance on humans rather than gods to determine earthly events.

Te, or human virtue, became the foundation of the mandate to rule. It was an important part of the checks and balances of Chinese governance for the next 3,000 years. Over time, this principle formed the basis of a reciprocal relationship between the ruler and the ruled. The ruler had the duty to care for and govern his subjects justly. In turn, the people justly ruled had the responsibility to work hard and give the ruler what he needed. Ethics and morality had thus been inserted into the fiber of Zhou society. To say the least, this was an astounding advance—brute force was replaced by the concepts of justice and mutual responsibility 3,000 years ago in ancient China.

Problems of Governance

The Zhou tribe, originating west of the Shang, established their ruling capital in Chang'an, near today's city of Xi'an. The Zhou, believing that the Shang had gone too far in their centralization of power, decided that a federation of states was a better way to rule. So a decentralized federation of semi-feudal city-states, based on strong family and tribal ties, became the political organization of the vast Chinese lands.

It was understood that the ruler would choose high ministers from his immediate family. But intermarriage among noble families enabled important positions to be given to other individuals— thereby shoring up support for the ruler and facilitating the relative equality of states within the Zhou federation. For example, King Wu married a Shang princess as his principal wife, thus raising her family to the status of advisers and ministers in his court along with his own Zhou family members.

In the early years of the Zhou dynasty, when people still remembered the horrors of the Shang tyrants, the rulers were reasonably benevolent. Ruling families whose members had intermarried worked together in the same city-states. Eventually, however, this cooperative spirit began to wane as noble families jockeyed for advantage over one another. Special problems arose when a young king died, leaving only a baby son as heir to the throne. By custom, the toddler king would sit on the throne while his mother, hidden behind a curtain, told him what to say in conducting the affairs of state. (The mother, in turn, was supposed to receive instructions from the regent, typically the deceased king's oldest living brother.) Until the child grew up, he was effectively a puppet playing the part of king. Unscrupulous family members of the mother's clan typically took advantage of this temporary power vacuum to raid the treasury and carry out all sorts of political intrigues. Upon reaching

This page from *Lives of the Emperors* shows a Zhou ruler riding in a chariot. The first Zhou rulers were fair and just, but eventually competition for power led to corruption and abuses by the noble families.

adulthood and receiving actual power, the king might banish his mother's entire family. But the palace intrigues could start anew when he married and his wife's family became privileged. In this environment, friction was a constant.

Ambitions for more land and riches were satisfied initially with conquests to the south. The Zhou realm expanded to all reaches of the Yangtze River, and the conquests spread "Chinese-style" culture and technology. Eventually, however, the states in the Zhou federation turned on each other. Chicanery and warfare became the trend. In 771 B.C. King You was killed, leaving only weak sons as heirs. The new king escaped to the east, and a new capital was established at Luoyang, in the northern part of what is today Henan Province. Because the Zhou rule before and after this event differed so much, historians divide the dynasty into two periods: the Western Zhou and the Eastern Zhou. During the 400 years of the Eastern Zhou period, the nobles fought continually over which clan would receive the Mandate of Heaven to rule.

Social and Cultural Advances

In contrast to the social strife and chaos characteristic of the Shang era that came before and the Eastern Zhou that came after, the Western Zhou was a time of relative restraint, cooperation, and benign culture. Although slavery was not outlawed, it was discouraged, and the wholesale enslaving of conquered tribes and commoners who could not pay their taxes stopped. The practice of human sacrifice seems to have ceased as well, though animal sacrifices continued intermittently in the early years of the dynasty.

The Zhou decided that if the peasant farmers were treated well and not overtaxed to the point of starvation, they would become more prosperous—and in the end, the state would actually gain more in tax revenues. The late Neolithic method of taxing in kind, rather than in money, was reinstated. The king's lands were parceled out to loyal nobles, who in turn parceled out their land to groups of commoners to farm. Throughout the kingdom there was a standard-size square of land, which was divided into nine smaller squares. Eight peasant families were each assigned an outer square. The inner square was farmed by all, and its produce was turned over to the noble. This is called "well farming" since the tic-tac-toe lines marking the fields look like the Chinese character for "well." Taxation and the division of lands were thus made fairer and more regulated by rules instead of by favoritism and family connections.

Although the nobles still enjoyed hunting parties, they were confined to royal parks set aside for this purpose so that the horses

During the Western Zhou period, warfare was largely restricted to less accessible spaces, as farmland was too valuable to destroy. This encouraged the development of the martial arts. In this photo, modern-day practitioners of tai chi, a discipline based on martial arts movements, go through the motions on the Great Wall of China.

would not trample valuable growing fields. Petty war continued, but because almost all flat land was now protected for farming (and thus the generation of tax revenues), the style of Shang warfare—with massive chariots devastating the enemy and the countryside on the broad plains—was no longer acceptable. Skirmishes were now more likely to occur in less accessible places, where hand-to-hand combat was more effective. The martial arts had their early origins in Western Zhou interstate warfare.

In almost every way, the life of commoners improved under Western Zhou rule. The basic culinary pattern of rice or other cooked grain, flavored with small savories of cut meats and vegetables, became available to nearly all people. This is still the basis of the nutritious Chinese diet today. Home construction was improved, creating more comfortable and healthful living conditions for the vast majority of ordinary people. Nearly all homes were now built above ground, with a wooden frame holding a glazed tile roof and tamped earth for walls. Only the very poor still lived in pit houses with thatched roofs.

Bronze making was still monopolized by the ruling classes, but the fierce monster decorations characteristic of the Shang changed to softer, more intricate designs. Extensive writings on oracle bones were replaced by long statements on bronze ritual vessels; such statements explained the special events commemorated by the vessel.

The most important cultural advance by the Western Zhou was in literature. Zhou scholars were sent around the kingdom to collect the legends and tales of the worthy heroes and admirable events of the past as well as the present. This led to the collection of 305 short poems called the *Shijing* (*Book of Songs*). Evidently this compilation was immensely popular in its day, serving as a source of inspiration for singers and for the educated in their moments of relaxation and

The Duke of Zhou

The duke of Zhou is one of the most revered people in all of Chinese history. When King Wu died only seven years after overthrowing the Shang dynasty, he left his 13-year-old son, Cheng, as his heir. As was the custom then, the duke of Zhou—as the deceased king's oldest living brother—became regent, ruling until the boy king came of age. The duke's younger brothers, seeking to enlarge their own states and suspecting the duke of having designs on the throne, rose up in rebellion. The duke put down the rebellion and for the next seven years ruled wisely and well.

When Cheng Wang (*wang* means "king") reached 20, he should have begun his rule. But the duke did not step aside. Instead he completed the reconstruction of the capital, which had been wrecked in the overthrow of the Shang king. The duke ordered that special care be taken with the Bright Hall, the temple of public ceremony.

At the end of the year, the duke summoned all the nobles of the realm to help consecrate the Bright Hall in its opening ceremonies. Assigned to the nearby ancestor

reflection. The poems, which are still popular, provide a picture of what life was like, particularly for the common people, so many years ago.

Even more important was the creation of the *I Ching* (*Book of Changes*). Tradition has it that this mystical book was created during the seven years when King Wu's father, Ji Chang, was imprisoned by the cruel last Shang king. During his captivity, Ji Chang wrote a treatise in which he intermixed the relationship among heaven, the earth, and the people into 64 hexagrams, thus producing the *I Ching*, a book that would replace the oracle bones

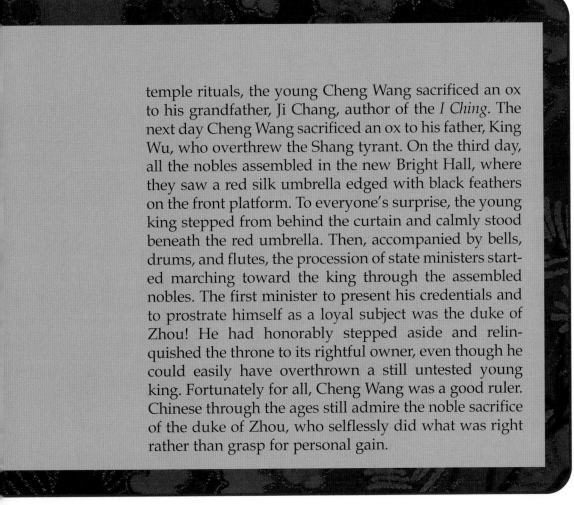

temple rituals, the young Cheng Wang sacrificed an ox to his grandfather, Ji Chang, author of the *I Ching*. The next day Cheng Wang sacrificed an ox to his father, King Wu, who overthrew the Shang tyrant. On the third day, all the nobles assembled in the new Bright Hall, where they saw a red silk umbrella edged with black feathers on the front platform. To everyone's surprise, the young king stepped from behind the curtain and calmly stood beneath the red umbrella. Then, accompanied by bells, drums, and flutes, the procession of state ministers started marching toward the king through the assembled nobles. The first minister to present his credentials and to prostrate himself as a loyal subject was the duke of Zhou! He had honorably stepped aside and relinquished the throne to its rightful owner, even though he could easily have overthrown a still untested young king. Fortunately for all, Cheng Wang was a good ruler. Chinese through the ages still admire the noble sacrifice of the duke of Zhou, who selflessly did what was right rather than grasp for personal gain.

of earlier generations for predicting the future. To foretell the future, six sticks were tossed, and the resulting pattern was matched to a hexagram of six full or broken lines displayed in the *I Ching*. Each pattern had a specified significance.

Over the years, various sages added extensive explanations and commentaries to the hexagram patterns in the *I Ching*. "Casting the *I Ching*" to divine the future remains very popular even today.

The overthrow of the Western Zhou dynasty in 771 B.C. plunged China into more than 500 years of chaos and strife. This jade disk decorated with dragons, created during the Warring States period (475–221 B.C.), is now on display at the Municipal Museum of Luoyang, Henan Province.

6

Eastern Zhou: Chaos and Solutions

In 771 B.C. a coalition of nomad tribes and discontented nobles staged a coup against the reigning Zhou monarch, King You. King You was nothing like the upright King Wu or duke of Zhou of earlier times. Rather, he was self-absorbed and foolish. To impress his favorite concubine, he caused the palace alarm beacons to be lit. The Zhou army instantly mobilized and prepared to fight. When it became known that You's frivolous concubine was clapping her hands with glee at how much power her royal lover possessed, the disgusted soldiers returned to their barracks.

Hearing of the incident, the rebels mounted an attack on the capital to take advantage of King You's poor judgment. This time, when the king lit the alarm beacons in earnest, the army—assuming that another prank was being played—did not mobilize. As a result, the rebels won an easy victory, and King You was assassinated. But the rebels were suddenly afraid that the gods might punish them for deposing a legitimate (albeit childish) ruler, so they selected the weakest of You's sons and pronounced him the new king of Zhou. Fearing that he would be assassinated next, the new king moved his capital far to the east to Luoyang (about halfway between today's Xi'an and Shanghai).

Conflict and Chaos

The Eastern Zhou era is divided into two periods. The Spring and Autumn period is the name given to the first of these, covering the years 770–476 B.C. The term comes from *The Spring and Autumn Annals*, a book documenting events of the time in the state of Lu (the home of the philosopher Confucius) as well as other major Chinese states. During the Spring and Autumn period, central authority broke down. Although nominally still the ruling dynasty, the Zhou had neither the will nor the power to govern their vast lands, which fragmented into hundreds of city-states. Warfare erupted as the dukes who ruled the various city-states sought to expand their power at the expense of neighbors.

Eventually, seven powerful kingdoms emerged from the many local and regional conflicts. By annexing the territory of conquered rivals and by controlling the affairs of weaker states, these kingdoms between them gained actual control over the bulk of the territory in the Zhou realm. But this did not mean an end to the chaos and warfare, as the great states set about battling one another for supremacy over a 250-year period known as the Warring States period (475–221 B.C.). As with the Spring and Autumn period, this designation came from the title of a book—*Strategies of the Warring States*, which described the rulers and the strategies they used to defeat their opponents.

The Western Zhou had been concerned about building prosperity from the ground up. They believed that prosperous peasants ensured a prosperous state. Such enlightened goals were forgotten in the chaos of the Eastern Zhou era. Affairs of state increasingly were overwhelmed by the quest for victory in battle.

The nature of warfare, too, changed during Eastern Zhou times. Under the Western Zhou, warfare had been relatively chivalrous. Battles were carefully controlled contests to decide rivalries among feudal lords. In the early years of the Spring and Autumn period, warfare was still relatively courtly. The tale is told of the Battle of the River Hong, in 638 B.C., which pitted the duke of Song against the duke of Chu. While the latter's soldiers were crossing the river, they were surprised by the Song army, which could easily have annihilated them in this vulnerable position. But the duke of Song refused to give the signal to attack until Chu's soldiers had safely crossed the river and were assembled in battle formation. Song lost the battle, but the duke was not killed. When asked why he had not attacked when his enemy was in the river, he replied that the true sage does not crush the weak or order an attack until the opponent has formed its battle lines. At the time, the story was told with admiration for the duke of Song, who had upheld the ideals of fair play and nobility in battle.

By the end of the chaotic Warring States period, this sort of gallantry had been replaced by a philosophy of victory by any means—and by merciless treatment of the vanquished. Earlier, the soldiers of a defeated army were typically spared after a battle; when the losing side conceded defeat, the contested issue was considered settled, and often the soldiers who had not fallen in battle simply went home. Now defeated armies were annihilated.

During the Warring States period, warfare was increasingly the domain of professional commanders and soldiers with no firm allegiance to a particular ruler. The best military strategists hired themselves out to the highest-paying states. In the pursuit of victory, these commanders often made use of deception and sought to exploit the weaknesses of human nature. Their ideas were recorded in numerous military manuals, at least seven of which survive today. The most famous of these treatises, Sun Tzu's *Art of War*, demonstrates a profound grasp of human psychology; it continues to be studied by military professionals as well as business executives looking to gain an advantage over their competitors.

Like the elite generals, many noblemen during the Warring States period were willing—for the right price—to fight for any ruler. These highborn mercenaries contributed private chariots along with a personal retinue of paid foot soldiers drawn from the ranks of commoners. Many knights-for-hire were stateless nobles who had been pushed out of their territories by stronger neighbors.

New technology also gave a more desperate character to warfare during the Warring States period. The invention of cast iron (apparently accomplished through modification of the bronze casting process) enabled stronger, sharper, and deadlier weapons to be produced. Iron projectile tips proved particularly lethal in combination with another new invention, the crossbow. Operating a crossbow required comparatively little training, so armies of commoners could be mobilized and prepared for a fight very quickly. In battle, a massed group of crossbowmen could discharge a deadly rain of iron-tipped arrows on the enemy—all the while remaining safely out of range of hand-to-hand combat with spears or knives. There is evidence that large factories for the manufacture of crossbow pivot releases produced thousands of standardized mechanisms for these weapons.

But it wasn't simply the more lethal weapons that led to wholesale slaughter during the Warring States period. Victorious armies took to massacring defeated soldiers in part to prevent mercenaries from once again hiring themselves out to a rival state in the future. The color red and the element fire now seemed to fit the Zhou

Two Chinese blacksmiths manufacture iron tools. The invention of cast iron during the Warring States period put stronger, sharper, and deadlier weapons into the hands of warriors, but it also helped make farmers more productive.

dynasty, though the king of Zhou was by this time the ruler of only a tiny, inconsequential state—and was king in name only.

The constant bloodshed and perpetual chaos stood in sharp contrast to the relative peace that had prevailed in the former federation of states under Western Zhou rule. Sages and ministers lamented the evils of their time and longed for a return to the more civilized ideals of that bygone age. Some recognized that the only way peace and stability could be restored would be for one of the major states to defeat all of its rivals.

Society and Culture in a Time of Disorder

Conflicts notwithstanding, the Eastern Zhou era saw significant advances in society and culture. The new technology of iron casting, in particular, brought benefits to ordinary people. In the past,

These bronze Chinese coins date from the Warring States period.

metal had been reserved for the powerful ruling class, but iron was less expensive and easier to make than bronze, and soon farmers and laborers were using iron plows and small iron tools. Iron plows, tillers, and harvest implements—along with the use of oxen as draft animals—made farming much easier and more productive. And with the increase in food production, the population grew rapidly. Because bronze no longer had the same military significance, expensive copper ore was now made into coins, replacing the cowry shell money of old.

Nevertheless, taxation became more onerous as nobles sought to raise the ever-increasing amounts of money necessary to hire armies to fight their rivals. It is estimated that the states of Chu and Qin could field armies of a million hired soldiers each.

There was no longer an ongoing, centralized program of public-works projects, and roads, bridges, and dams fell apart if they were not useful for military purposes. The worst problem, though, was that basic security was virtually nonexistent. Destructive armies and incessant warfare meant that fields and villages were no longer protected by a powerful state. Many peasants left their exposed villages and went to the walled cities as laborers, dislocating families and village life even more; many others became hired soldiers.

Sages and state ministers, like the peasants, were affected by the turmoil. In the past, they had lived comfortable lives in the royal palaces, where they organized the rituals, wrote the official histories, and advised the rulers on matters of state. Now most of these sages were out of a job because rulers let the administration of their realms take a backseat to military affairs. Even the nine bronze tripods of the emperor Yu—the symbols of rule—somehow got lost in all the chaos and confusion. Many a sage was forced to become a sort of itinerant consultant, traveling from state to state in an effort to convince a noble to employ his knowledge services.

A Flowering of Philosophy

In spite of—or perhaps because of—the chaos and conflict, the Eastern Zhou was a period of amazing philosophical inquiry. Chinese thinkers examined humanity's place in the world and offered a range of ideas regarding the basis of a good and just society. The most famous of these thinkers, known in the West as Confucius, was born around the middle of the sixth century B.C. An

The teachings of Confucius would have a great impact on 2,500 years of Chinese culture. This portrait of the famous sage is stamped in red ink on paper.

Confucius: Hierarchy of Obedience and Mutual Respect

Confucius, who would become China's most influential political and moral philosopher centuries after his death, was born around 551 B.C. into the Kong family, deposed nobles in the state of Lu in eastern China. (The name Confucius is actually an Anglicized version of Kong Fuzi, meaning "Master Kong.") His parents had fallen onto relatively hard times, and his father, a knight-for-hire, died when the boy was quite young.

The Lu state was known for its preservation of the rituals and traditions of the early Zhou era, and Confucius earned a reputation for the conscientious performance of traditional rituals, for politeness, and for a love of learning. He started a school for sages in his home state, but when he was about 35, Lu fell to a rival noble and Confucius fled. For the next 20 years he tried to establish a career as a state adviser, but he was not markedly successful. He finally abandoned the

itinerant sage-administrator who believed in the critical role of learning, he established a school for young sages. Although largely ignored during his lifetime, the teachings of Confucius would be tremendously influential in later Chinese culture. Confucius saw proper social relations as highly hierarchical, though reciprocal responsibility and respect should govern the behavior of all, regardless of their rank. Rulers, for example, should govern by virtue and moral example rather than by force or strictly by laws. Subjects should exercise self-control and be obedient to the just ruler. All should act out of a regard for what is right rather than out

civil service and wandered from state to state, followed by his disciples. He eventually returned to Lu, where he died in 479 B.C.

Confucius's principles of personal behavior, many of which are found in *The Analects*, a book compiled by his disciples, include honoring one's parents, being kind and polite to others, and doing what is right rather than what is merely personally advantageous. Confucius also enunciated a version of the Golden Rule: don't do to others what you wouldn't want for yourself. In the area of governance, he supported the concept of a divine mandate to rule but believed that rulers must lead by good moral example rather than by resorting to force. For every person — whether subject or ruler, child or parent, younger sibling or older — obedience to proper authority, self-control, and respect were the most important duties in Confucius's conception of the proper hierarchical social order.

of self-interest. Significantly, Confucius had no place for war in his ideal society.

Lao-tzu (also spelled Lao Tze and Laozi) is traditionally credited as the founder of Taoism (Daoism), a mystical—and somewhat difficult to define—philosophy that would have a huge impact throughout China, Southeast Asia, and beyond. Some Chinese sources say he was a contemporary of Confucius, though modern scholars debate whether Lao-tzu was actually a historical figure. In any case, Taoism in broad terms emphasized harmony with nature and regarded complex social patterns and secular ambition as unnatural human folly.

This painting in a Taoist temple shows Lao-tzu being offered food and money. Little is known for certain about the life of Lao-tzu—not even whether the sage credited as the founder of Taoism was a specific person or a combination of several people blended into one semi-mythical figure. Most traditional sources, however, say he was born Li Erh around 604 B.C. and died in 531 B.C.

It taught that people should live in harmony with the universe by abandoning themselves to the eternal path, or Tao, of natural virtue (*Te*).

Mo Ti (Mozi), who lived during the fifth century B.C., taught that human beings naturally do what they believe is right, and thus moral education can play a key role in promoting ethical behavior. Mo Ti and his followers, called Mohists, believed that morally correct actions are those that promote the welfare of all members of society. They advocated strong, even authoritarian governance but condemned waste and luxury and believed that rulers must be virtuous. The proper social order, in the view of the Mohists, was one that excluded conflict and especially military aggression.

Han Feizi, a Chinese philosopher of the third century B.C., developed a school of thought that is termed Legalism. Unlike Mohism, which assumed that human beings naturally do what they think is right, Legalism held that people behave badly unless they fear punishment or covet a reward. The Legalists did not look for a benevolent, virtuous ruler to lead by moral example, as did the Confucianists, but rather for a leader who maintained the social order by strictly and uniformly enforcing clear, rational laws. Severe, certain punishment for transgressions, as well as rewards for cooperation, should be handed out regardless of an individual's social status or family connections.

All of these currents in Chinese thought may be seen as attempts to outline the basis of a social order free from the strife and chaos that afflicted the Eastern Zhou dynasty. Such a development, however, would not take place until one of the warring states emerged as the preeminent power.

During the Qin dynasty (221–206 B.C.), existing defensive walls along China's northwestern border were combined to form the Great Wall of China. When the project was finished, the wall stretched from Linzhao (Gansu Province) in the west to Liaodong (Jilin Province) in the east.

7

Qin: The First Unified Empire

During the Warring States period, many people fervently hoped that a powerful king would emerge to unite China and usher in a great new age of peace and stability. Few would have predicted that this king would hail from the small northwestern state of Qin. Situated between the rest of China and the raiding "barbarian" tribes of the frontier, Qin was regarded as an uncouth buffer zone not worth much notice. The eastern states of Zhao, Wei, Han, Song, Qi, Yan, Chu, Lu, and Zhou thought of themselves as the repositories of Chinese culture and scholarship.

These civilized states hired sages and advisers who leaned toward modified Confucian ideals. For the most part the sages de-emphasized the ideal of humility and virtue expected of the ruler. Instead, they emphasized obedience to and respect for the king (to be exhibited

Han Feizi: Advocate of Legalism

Han Feizi (circa 280–233 B.C.) lived near the end of the tumultuous Warring States period. Born a prince of the noble Han family, he was educated in the Confucian tradition but ultimately rejected Confucius's ideas about governance based on the moral example of rulers and on the goodwill and reciprocal responsibility felt by the ruler and his ministers and subjects. Han Feizi observed that, under a naturally benevolent ruler, rule would be just; but under a ruler with a cruel personality, the people would likely suffer abuse. He also doubted that the people would live up to their responsibilities under a benevolent ruler; instead they would see that they could take advantage, and their tendencies toward laziness and dishonesty would emerge.

Han Feizi said that laws should be written down, made known to everyone, and enforced consistently. He suggested that there were two ways to ensure the people's obedience to the rules: harsh punishment for breaking the rules, and rewards for following them. He called these two tools of power the two handles.

Although his philosophy underpinned Qin rule, Han Feizi was imprisoned by the Qin king, after which he committed suicide.

by courtly rituals and protocol), along with the study of earlier—and, to their minds, more virtuous—times. The Qin state, however, had little interest in these traditions of ritual, politeness, and erudition. Legalism, very different from this prevailing Confucian Chinese thought, appealed more to the Qin.

In 352 B.C. the Qin king Xiaokong selected Shang Yang, a prominent early Legalist, as his prime minister. Shang Yang advised that if the ultimate goal was supremacy, the Qin ruler should alter the traditional social and administrative structure of his realm so that resources could be focused toward defeating militarily the other states. Shang Yang's approach was deeply pragmatic: the king, he counseled, should institute "whatever works." King Xiaokong ultimately enacted Shang Yang's five-point program:

1. *Redistribute the land.* Starting with unassigned land, and then encroaching on the hereditary nobles' productive domains, land was given directly to the peasants who farmed it (peasants were even permitted to buy and sell land). This simultaneously reduced the wealth of the nobles—thus making it less likely that they could successfully rise up against the king—and encouraged the peasants to make their land as productive as possible. Peasant prosperity, in turn, created wealth for the state that could be used to support a strong army.

2. *Divide the state into administrative districts.* This further undercut the power of the nobles (who had previously administered the realm for the king) and concentrated authority with the central government. It also ensured that the central government could collect more of the state's wealth for itself.

3. *Change the taxation system to break the traditional loyalty to family (and replace it with loyalty to the state).* Those homes that included two or more grown sons, for example, had to pay double tax.

4. *Establish a severe penal code based on collective responsibility.* Several families were organized into a group. If one

member of the group did wrong, the others were bound to turn the offender over to the authorities; otherwise they were all assigned the same punishment (typically violent death, regardless of the infraction).

5. *Establish a merit system whereby those who distinguished themselves in war would be rewarded.* A nobleman who failed to distinguish himself in battle lost his noble status, a fact that was surely an incentive to fight bravely. Commoners in the army—a universal draft of 15-year-olds supplied a huge fighting force of crossbow-bearing foot soldiers—were motivated by the promise of more freedom and the possibility of advancement and prosperity. And because the state of Qin had more iron deposits than other states, it was able to outfit its army with more effective iron swords and crossbows, giving Qin an advantage in battle.

Qin Shi Huang Di was the first emperor of a unified China. This drawing is from a 19th-century Korean album.

After the implementation of Lord Shang's five-point program, the centralized wealth of the Qin state grew steadily over the next 100 years. And paralleling that increase in wealth was a rise in Qin military might (a major ingredient of which was its cavalry).

In 255 B.C. the Qin king Zhaoxiang defeated the last Zhou king in the

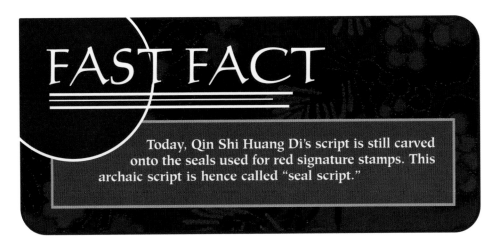

FAST FACT

Today, Qin Shi Huang Di's script is still carved onto the seals used for red signature stamps. This archaic script is hence called "seal script."

capital of Luoyang. Because the Zhou had remained—in theory if not in fact—China's ruling dynasty, Zhaoxiang assumed that his victory meant he could now claim rulership over all of China. But just as they had long ignored the weak Zhou rulers, the other states now ignored the upstart Qin. It was clear to the Qin that they must also conquer all the other states to enforce their claim on China.

It took just 23 years for the Qin war machine to vanquish one state after another under Zheng, the next Qin king. Fear of "the Qin Tiger," as Zheng became known, was so great that in 221 B.C., the final two states gave up without a fight.

Founding of the Qin Dynasty

After the capitulation of the last warring state, Qi, King Zheng established the new Qin dynasty and, as was the custom, changed his name. Recalling the name of the legendary Yellow Emperor—Huang Di—Zheng dubbed himself Shi Huang Di (pronounced "sher-hwahng-der"), the "First High Emperor."

The new emperor set about centralizing authority in all of China, as his forefathers had earlier done in the state of Qin. First, Qin Shi Huang Di dismantled China's feudal structure. He built a grand new capital in Xianyang (near today's Xi'an) and made the former rulers of each of the conquered states move there so that he could keep an eye on them. The later historian Sima Qian wrote that an exact replica of each ruler's palace was built in a vast, carefully guarded park. There the former rulers and lesser nobles could entertain one another and play, but they were not allowed to rule their conquered states. Their weapons were melted down and recast into bells, statues, and other harmless objects. In all, some 120,000 families were moved to Qin Shi Huang Di's guarded park.

Everyone was declared equal under the law. Hereditary titles were abolished, and all land that had formerly belonged to the elite was redistributed to the peasants, who paid their taxes to the central treasury.

The emperor divided the realm into 36 major districts called commanderies (*jun*) and assigned a loyal Qin administrator to each. Each commandery was further divided into counties (*xian*). Recommendations, orders, and reports were required to be in writing, and the volume of bamboo-strip writing traveling back and forth between the 36 commanderies and the capital was apparently staggering. It was said that the emperor himself—as hard a worker as any of his administrators—would not retire for the night until he had processed 120 pounds of reports and memos over the course of the day.

Qin Shi Huang Di was guided by seven principles for rulers that had been enunciated by the Legalist philosopher Han Feizi:

1. Know and compare all the various possibilities.

2. Punish failure with unvarying severity to discourage others from breaking the law.

3. Grant generous and reliable rewards for success.

4. Listen to all views, and hold the proposer responsible for every word.

Qin Shi Huang Di orders that books be burned and scholars thrown into a deep ravine in this illustration from *Lives of the Emperors*.

5. Issue unfathomable orders and make deceptive assignments to keep potential enemies under control.

6. Conceal one's own knowledge when making enquiries of a minister; that way you can see if you are being lied to.

7. Speak in opposites and act in contraries to keep the element of surprise in your own sphere.

The emperor promulgated a written code of law, similar to the one that had helped transform the small Qin state into China's greatest power. The new code replaced all other laws in the empire. It was detailed and harsh. Citizens were expected to inform on their neighbors and even family members if a law were broken. Criticizing the law was punishable by death.

Qin Shi Huang Di intended to make his dynasty so great and powerful that it would last forever. In 213 B.C., at a banquet for the emperor, a guest suggested that previous dynasties had lasted for centuries because they had adhered to old traditions. This was taken not simply as a criticism of the emperor's break with tradition, but also as an implication that the Qin dynasty would not last. Li Si, the emperor's Legalist prime minister, replied to the imprudent speaker that the past must not be used to discredit the present. And the dinner conversation provoked an event that would arouse bitter resentment among Chinese people through the ages: Qin Shi Huang Di decreed that the works of the past, especially the literature compiled and written by the Zhou Confucian scholars, be destroyed. He put a death sentence on anyone who hid, or even quoted, the ancient writings. He sent his police throughout the empire, with orders to burn any book they found except for practical how-to manuals on agriculture and medicine. When Confucian scholars refused to let their libraries be burned, they were beheaded, buried alive, or, if lucky, sent to work as slaves on the Great Wall—and their books were set to flames anyway. So the empire, whose dynasty took the color black and the element water, was finally stabilized. The peace,

A bronze Qin-era coin with a square hole in the center. Coins like this one remained in use in China until the 20th century.

however, was maintained only through strict and brutal control.

Foundations for the Future

Qin Shi Huang Di was a consummate administrator. He realized that his empire would work smoothly only if everything of importance were standardized, from the central capital to the farthest border post. He made the Qin version of writing the official one. This enabled all reports and orders to be processed without the need for translators and special scribes. Qin Shi Huang Di standardized the measures to be used throughout the empire, which facilitated the collection and recording of taxes and improved trade throughout the vast lands. The emperor minted round coins with square cutouts in the center, which made the coins easy to string and minimized the amount of metal needed; these coins remained in use in China into the early 20th century. He built roads throughout the empire to improve communication and trade, and he even set the width of wheel axles so that all vehicles would fit on these roads. Qin Shi Huang Di's ideas regarding the importance of efficient administration provided the foundation for the characteristic imperial Chinese bureaucracy of the next 2,100 years.

With the resources of a vast empire to draw on, and with virtually unlimited power over his subjects, Qin Shi Huang Di could think big. A total of 700,000 workers spent his entire reign building his tomb and sculpting a vast terra-cotta army to guard him in the afterlife. Vast amounts of materials and labor were expended on construction of the new capital and the royal park of palaces, and providing for the day-to-day living expenses of the tens of thousands who lived there must have consumed incredible treasure. Qin Shi Huang Di had 1,000 divers search a river for the legendary *dings* of Yu—which were rumored to have fallen into that river during the Warring States period—but the ancient bronze tripods were never found. More than 1,250 miles of canals, many of them still used today, were dug to improve communication. New roads and

(continued on p. 88)

Death and the First Emperor

The man who first unified China in a single empire was clever, cunning, ruthless, and—particularly toward the end of his life—morbidly afraid of dying. Part of that fear may have stemmed from an assassination attempt that nearly succeeded.

The man who would eventually give himself the title Shi Huang Di—the "First High Emperor—was born Zheng in 259 B.C. His parentage is somewhat murky—while officially acknowledged as the son of a Qin prince and a dancing girl, his actual father may have been a merchant. At age 13 Zheng became king of Qin.

As king, Zheng continued the work of his forebears in conquering the other Chinese states. Eventually the rival Yan state hatched a plan to assassinate the leader of Qin, a plot author John Wills Jr. describes in his book *Mountain of Fame: Portraits in Chinese History*. Many years earlier, a Qin general had defected to Yan, and his hatred of Zheng was so great that he now offered his own head to make the assassination plot work. The Yan swordsman Jing Ke would go to Zheng and pretend he was a traitor. He would bring a bundle of rolled up maps and offer to show King Zheng the best strategic positions for an attack on the Yan state. Inside the maps the swordsman would hide his unsheathed sword. To convince the king of his sincerity, Jing Ke would present Zheng with the general's head.

The gift of the general's head had its intended effect, and Jing Ke gained admittance into the great hall of King Zheng. As the false traitor began making his presentation, he suddenly drew his sword from the rolled-up maps. The first blow missed, and Zheng ran behind the pillars. The palace guards were quickly summoned, and they cut down the would-be assassin.

After that episode, Zheng seems to have become increasingly obsessed with, and fearful of, death. As Emperor Qin Shi Huang Di, he set vast gangs of laborers to building the largest mausoleum ever constructed in China. Meanwhile, he dispatched his ministers on numerous journeys to find the secret of immortality. According to Sima Qian, one of these ministers returned and told him, "When you are in the palace, do not let others know where you are." According to the historian, this was supposed to prevent evil spirits from being able to find the emperor (though it would also thwart potential assassins). Qin Shi Huang Di turned his various palaces into mazes of secret corridors, walkways, and towers. If someone revealed where the emperor was at any time, that person was put to death.

Finally, in 210 B.C., the emperor was informed that if he were to catch a certain magic fish, he would become immortal. Qin Shi Huang Di, his son, and Prime Minister Li Si took off with a great entourage, ostensibly to make an inspection tour of the empire. The emperor died in his sleep en route. In order to have time to hatch their plans of succession, the minister and son kept the death a secret and pretended the emperor wanted his privacy. Since Qin Shi Huang Di was well known by this time for his odd behavior, the emperor's absence from view was easily accepted. But on the long journey back to the capital, the corpse began to stink. So the plotters bought some wagonloads of fish and placed these around the royal carriage, stating that the emperor had now taken a fancy to the odor. Today, when a Chinese says, "That smells like rotten fish," he or she means that a big deception is going on.

These are some of the thousands of terra-cotta warriors that were buried about 2,200 years ago to guard the tomb of Emperor Qin Shi Huang Di. Chinese peasants digging a well in the 1970s stumbled upon the statues near Xi'an. The emperor's tomb has yet to be fully excavated.

bridges, all of the same width to accommodate the standardized carts and wagons, crisscrossed the land.

But the most enormous project of all was the 1,500-mile-long Great Wall. This massive wall, studded with beacon towers, was built to keep out nomadic raiders from the Gobi Desert in the north. Hundreds of thousands of laborers were conscripted to work on the project, and way out on the edge of the desert, conditions were appalling. Soon work on the wall was considered a death sentence, so criminals were added to the ranks of the unfortunate conscripted laborers. Taskmasters were unconcerned about living conditions, since they could count on more criminals arriving each day. And in the event that too many laborers fell, the foremen would simply kidnap those who delivered food and water. When workers on the supply trains grew wary of completing their deliveries, villages were raided for able-bodied men to continue building the wall. In all, it is estimated that more than 100,000 men perished over the course of the project. Their bodies were simply tossed into the foundation of the next portion of the wall because no time was allowed for proper burial. Poems lamenting the loss of husbands and sons sent to work on the wall survive to this day.

As his reign progressed, Shi Huang Di became obsessed with avoiding his own death. He began to exhibit bizarre behavior, gradually withdrawing from other people and losing his sense of reality. In 210 B.C., only 11 years after he began his reign as emperor, Qin Shi Huang Di died on an expedition in search of the secret of immortality. Keeping the death a secret until he could work out the succession to his own advantage, the Legalist minister Li Si tricked Qin Shi Huang Di's capable older son into committing suicide. This left the younger son to take the place as the second Qin emperor, Er Shi.

Er Shi was as cruel as his father, but he lacked Qin Shi Huang Di's brilliant gift for administration. As soon as Er Shi had murdered Li Si and his father's other ministers, he installed his own favorites and began a career of oppression and waste. Tax levies were raised so high, and brutal punishments became so commonplace, that peasants began to flee to the mountains. There they formed bands of brigands and plotted to overthrow the Qin dynasty.

In the end, however, Er Shi's prime minister, Zhao Gao, disposed of the emperor through trickery. Realizing that Er Shi was secretly afraid for his own sanity, Zhao Gao brought a deer to the palace but forced all the courtiers to say it was a horse. Convinced now that he was hallucinating, Er Shi retired to a distant palace for some rest. Zhao Gao hired actors to impersonate a group of rebel bandits and descend on the palace, and there, in 207 B.C., Er Shi either committed suicide in a panic or was murdered.

Qin Shi Huang Di's grandson became the third Qin emperor, but his reign lasted only 46 days. Real rebels had marched on the capital, and they put a definitive end to the Qin dynasty. The first Chinese imperial dynasty, which Qin Shi Huang Di had dreamed would rule forever, had endured for only 15 years.

These bronze figures of cavalry soldiers date to the later years of the Han dynasty.

8

Early Han: A Flowering of Culture

By the year 207 B.C., revolts against the brutal Qin dynasty were springing up in all parts of the empire. A combined force of rebels was advancing on the Qin capital. The old nobility rallied under the former aristocrat Xiang Yu, who hoped to reinstate the feudal system. Common people and bandits who sought an end to forced labor and ruinous taxes followed the charismatic Liu Bang, an uneducated peasant. Initially both forces worked together. They defeated the Qin, and the grateful Han state awarded Liu Bang the title Prince of Han.

Soon after the fall of the Qin capital, however, the two leaders turned on each other. What followed was almost five years of civil war. Although the noble Xiang Yu had a better army and won more battles, he did not count on the great numbers of downtrodden peasants who continually joined Liu Bang's popular army of commoners. In the end, numbers overwhelmed skill, and Xiang Yu gave up the fight. In 202 B.C., Liu Bang took the name Gao Zu and became the Han dynasty emperor.

Reversing the Tyranny of the Qin

Emperor Gao Zu immediately began to roll back the oppressive practices of the Legalist Qin tyrants. He granted a general amnesty for all the combatants during the rebellion and sent everyone home. He pardoned Xiang Lu's family and the conquered Qin ministers and administrators; he even provided tomb maintenance for the last Qin emperor. Gao Zu eliminated wasteful court expenses and thus was able to lower taxes. In the legal sphere, he freed the slaves created by the Qin penal system. He also did away with the law that required families to inform on each other and eliminated the practice of punishing groups of families for the crime of a single person in the group.

The new emperor built a new capital at Chang'an (at today's Xi'an in Shaanxi Province). This Han capital would remain the capital of China until the Mongols conquered the land more than 1,000 years later.

Gao Zu never learned to read or write, and he distrusted intellectuals. He did tolerate discussion, however, and eliminated the Qin practice of swift death for anyone who dared criticize laws or policies. Although his practical nature favored the administrative aspects of Legalism, he had learned firsthand how dangerous the extremes of Legalism could be. He noticed that many people received comfort from the ideas of Confucianism, so he opened the door to Confucianist scholars without making Confucianism the official creed. Accepting it as a system of ethics and reciprocal benevolence, the early Han ministers freely adjusted the teachings to support pragmatic and efficient governance. A form of Taoism had also become popular with a few sages; this too was

This painting on silk shows kneeling prisoners and soldiers. It is part of a larger work titled *The First Emperor of the Han Dynasty Entering Kuan Tung*, by the 12th-century Chinese artist Chao Po-chu.

tolerated.

Under the capable and pragmatic administration of the early Han dynasty, the population flourished. In 2 B.C., the first Chinese census was taken. More than 57 million people were counted, at a time when the Roman Empire is estimated to have had only 7 million inhabitants.

Gao Zu restored the feudalism of the Zhou dynasty in a farsighted way. Although he could not avoid giving those who had fought with him lands and titles, these rewards came with restrictions designed to prevent the new nobles from becoming too strong and someday turning against Gao Zu's dynasty. When a noble died, his land had to be divided equally among all his sons. And when each of these sons died, their land in turn was divided equally among their sons. After several generations, many inheritances had been reduced to little more than family farms. Further division of the land resulted in plots that were too small to support a family, and

The Han emperor Wudi receives a letter in this illustration from *Lives of the Emperors*. Under Wudi, the Confucian system became the official basis of government in China.

at this point many people sold their meager landholdings and went to the cities to work for the state bureaucracy or, if they lacked education, on construction projects.

The educated civil service bureaucracy became a key underpinning of the new dynasty's rule. Instead of wasteful extravagances or expensive and destructive wars, the early Han court spent its taxes on a vast army of scholar-bureaucrats to administer the realm. Clerks were well trained and well supervised. Pay was decent, and for poor aristocrats who might otherwise be forced to work as menial laborers, civil service offered acceptable status.

The later emperor Wudi made Confucianism the state's official ideology and established the Imperial Academy to train new civil servants in Confucian principles. Wudi also started the system of state examinations, which were open to anyone who wished to advance into the administrative service.

Qin-style Legalism had failed in its promise of enabling effective rule whether the ruler was good or bad. Because it was too harsh, Legalism nearly destroyed the country, and it was forgotten. Administrative Confucianism, however, with its increasingly intricate hierarchies, tempered by ethics and morality, was to support the functioning of the Chinese imperial system throughout its long history. Emperor Gao Zu ruled only seven years before he died. The next 2,000 years saw many unremarkable, ineffective, or dissolute emperors and regents, but China and its army of bureaucrats carried on.

Expansion of Empire

Taking advantage of the civil war at the end of the Qin dynasty, northern Hun raiders had moved well south of the Great Wall, which had been built to keep them out of China. Gao Zu, the first Han emperor, led the army to beat the Huns back. He lost the battle and was taken captive. To regain his freedom, the emperor gave the Hun

Gao Zu, the Peasant Emperor

In 259 B.C. Liu Bang was born to a peasant family in Jiangsu Province, just north of today's coastal city of Shanghai. After a remarkable rags-to-riches life, he died in 195 B.C. as the first Han emperor Gao Zu. He is remembered as the leader who lifted the repression of the Qin tyrants. Through his shrewd policies, decisive actions, and innate tolerance, he set China on a path of prosperity, innovation, and cultural advancement that has rarely been equaled in history.

Liu Bang's biggest asset was a magnetic personality. Rather than farm for a living, he took low-level jobs in the Qin government that didn't require literacy. Eventually he was appointed foreman over a gang of 100 conscripted laborers at Qin Shi Huang Di's tomb. One morning, he noticed that half the workers had escaped during the night. He knew he would be a dead man once this was discovered, so he cut the rest of the workers loose and became a bandit. Several of those freed followed him. They become the first unit in the rebel army he soon raised to fight the Qin.

Liu Bang's rebel troops were the ones who finally defeated the Qin. In accepting the Qin surrender, Liu Bang spared the royal family's lives. A week later, however, a competing army reached the capital, slaughtered

chieftain a vast tribute and a Chinese princess in marriage. This set the pattern for the next half century. Han emperors avoided fighting the northern barbarians by sending tribute and royal hostages.

Emperor Wudi ruled from 141 to 87 B.C. Not much is known about him, but he seems to have had the personality of a tyrant, with fits of temper, extravagant tastes, and huge ambitions. He rejected the policy of sending riches and hostages to China's ene-

the Qin, and burned the palace. Liu Bang was so angry at this needless cruelty—which he considered as bad as the behavior of the former tyrants—that he resolved to take it upon himself to change China for the better. In the civil war that followed, Liu Bang proved himself a poor but lucky general: one account states that he lost every battle in which he personally commanded except the last one—and, of course, that was the one that counted. He himself said the secret of his success was that he selected the best talent he could find for each job, and he rewarded those who succeeded. This was unusual in a time when leaders were taught to cut down those with talent, who might be potential rivals.

Never educated, the feisty new emperor pretended to be even more uncouth than he actually was when dealing with the snobbish court sages. However, he consistently cultivated his connection with the common people. Gao Zu never forgot his humble roots and was forever proud that these people had made him their leader.

During an attack on an upstart noble, Gao Zu was struck by a stray arrow. Although the battle was won, Gao Zu's wound soon became infected. Within a month, the first Han emperor was dead.

mies. Instead, he resolved to conquer all the raiders once and for all. He mobilized the riches of China and focused his military on taking the offensive. What followed was an expansion of the empire in all directions. China expanded south to Vietnam and northeast to Korea. On the west, Wudi's envoys went as far as Samarkand (in present-day Uzbekistan), and possibly beyond.

Wudi established the tribute system, which was to remain in

force throughout the imperial era. Rather than attempt to directly rule his far-flung empire, Wudi negotiated a sort of vassal system, whereby the conquered state continued to rule itself but
gave allegiance to the Chinese emperor as a close ally. As part of
the Chinese sphere of influence, the conquered state was expected to adopt many of the Chinese ways (such as the Chinese written characters, for ease of communication). To cement the state's
subservience to the emperor, annual caravans of costly tribute
were delivered to the Chinese capital. In this way, raw materials
and luxuries the Chinese lacked were supplied to the empire,
and the Chinese Way was spread throughout much of the Asian
continent.

The crowning achievement of this expansion was the building of
the Silk Road. This was not literally a road, but a series of way sta-
tions and security treaties with the tribes along a vast trade route
extending through high deserts and mountain passes from the China
Sea to the Middle East. The Silk Road was always fraught with peril,
from the fierce elements to the fierce bandits. Nevertheless, it was
secure enough to carry a large volume of trade: silks and pearls were
transported west to the Roman Empire, and camels, horses, cobalt,
and metalworking technologies flowed back to the Han workshops
and merchants.

Flowering of Culture and Technology

Under the Han, China now had a society in which the best
chances for getting ahead went to intellectuals and those who
studied hard, rather than to members of the clergy, military, or
hereditary nobility. The Chinese believe that the successes and
failures of the past provide guidance for the present and the future.
Hence, the study of history is not a leisure activity, but a vital occu-
pation. The Han Confucian scholars were free to again look to the
past for guidance. But the nation had been robbed of its past. The

scholars understood with bitterness that the records of their ancestors had been burned by the Qin tyrants.

Sima Qian (145–87 B.C.) and his father resolved to restore the lost records. They traveled the empire, gathering up those few ancient books that had been hidden in walls or buried in yards or fields. Old people were interviewed and their memories of past events, along with stories told to them as children, were written down. To the Chinese, this reconstructing of their past was as vital as reconnecting a severed part of the body. Sima Qian completed his vast work, 130 volumes in all, using history-gathering techniques far in advance of those practiced in any other civilization of the time. Besides ancient writings (the hidden books that had escaped destruction), he sifted through numerous versions of the same stories told orally. He recorded the version that was most consistent with other events, common sense, and memories of the most credible persons interviewed. He was careful to point out what was speculative or legendary, and what was considered reliable reporting. Sima Qian's vast *Historical Records* (sometimes called *Records of the Grand Historian*) is so thorough and so credible that even today it is considered essential reading about ancient China. (An English translation from 1895 was used in researching this book.) In the last 100 years, archaeologists have proved the essential accuracy of much that Sima Qian recorded, and his history is considered an amazing scholarly accomplishment.

Literature and art flourished during the early Han era, which was an exciting time of cross-cultural exchange and increasing prosperity and peace. Paper was invented to facilitate the enormous administrative activity of the civil service. A revised script was developed that was better suited to the brush and ink materials used by the 130,000-odd clerks employed by the government. The world's first dictionary, *Shuo Wen* (Words Explained), was pro-

During the Han dynasty, paper was invented and a revised Chinese script created to facilitate record-keeping with brush and ink.

duced. It included the meaning and pronunciation of more than 9,000 Han "clerical script" Chinese characters. Porcelain was invented. Colorful paintings on silk detailed daily life in the palaces and estates. Imposing sculptures known as tomb guardians began to be placed outside ancestor tombs.

Among the numerous inventions and technological advances of the early Han period, a few stand out as especially amazing. For example, the Chinese discovered that natural gas seeped through cracks in the earth near their salt mines. Using bamboo rods, they piped this gas to streetlamps in the nearby towns for night illumination. Agriculture during early Han times was particularly advanced, to the point that one might call it agri-business. Plows, irrigation machines, wheelbarrows, threshers, and so forth helped landowners feed the expanding population. Crop rotation was introduced, making it unnecessary to let fields lie fallow in order to restore their fertility.

The early Han dynasty is recognized by later Chinese as the era when the essential pattern of Chinese government and Chinese culture was securely imprinted for the next 2,000 years.

9

Epilogue: Wang Mang— Heaven's Mandate, Gained and Lost

The glory of the Han dynasty and its modified Confucian "Chinese Way" was soon interrupted. Because of the grandiose schemes Emperor Wudi launched without cost control, the imperial coffers were emptied. Wudi made matters worse with shortsighted solutions. He debased the coinage, peddled civil service jobs, and sold titles for special tax-free estates. These new estates did not need to be split among sons after the owner's death. Thus, the number of large, tax-free estates increased. Rich officials and merchants even managed to acquire land from small peasant-owners, who now became rent-paying tenants. In this way the number of small peasant holdings paying taxes to the imperial treasury declined. As more and more peasants fell behind in their rents, many were forced to sell themselves or their children into slavery to pay off their debts. The conflict between landlords and tenants, along with the concentration of power in the hands of wealthy families, would become a major problem in Chinese history.

Five wasteful emperors followed Wudi, and the situation went from bad to worse. China's influence abroad dwindled to the point that the annual caravans of tribute stopped coming to the capital, and the foreign alliances became tenuous at best. Beginning in A.D. 1, child emperors held the throne. During that time, the country was actually ruled by a regent, Wang Mang. Wang Mang seems to have been a sincere reformer, though some historians of the day disparaged him to legitimize the later Han rebellion.

The Rise and Fall of Wang Mang

Wang Mang was a distant relative of the Han emperor, one of the so-called outside ruling elite. These were persons in the same clan as the emperor, who could be trusted to serve as regents for the years when a child emperor grew to adulthood. Wang Mang was known as an excellent and virtuous public official. After slave revolts in the state iron mines and general distress and brigandry among the dispossessed peasants, Wang Mang decided that radical reform was necessary to save the empire. In the year A.D. 9, with the approval of the Han ruling family, he deposed the latest boy king and declared himself the founder of the Xin (New) dynasty, the recipient of the Mandate of Heaven to rule.

Wang Mang launched a program of major reforms designed to remedy the plight of the peasants and to increase the government's tax income. He lowered the salaries of civil servants and decreed that all land was now the property of the state. He divided up the

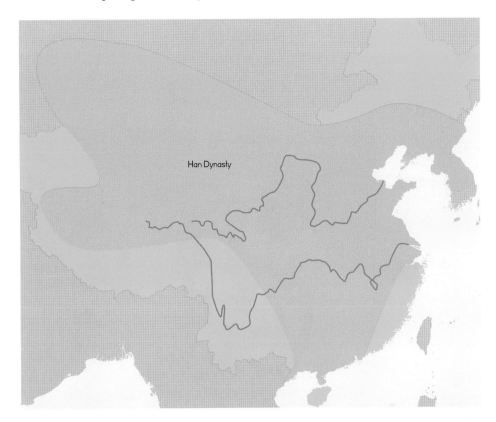

Han Dynasty

At its height the Han empire stretched from the Korean Peninsula in the northeast through Mongolia, Tibet, and part of central Asia in the west; it reached as far south as present-day northern Vietnam.

confiscated estates among peasant families, who would pay taxes to the emperor. He ordered that all gold be brought to the treasury and exchanged for bronze coins. He levied an income tax on merchants. He installed price controls on basic commodities in an attempt to control the inflation that had been ravaging family income during the preceding years. He also installed price supports, buying excess grain in good harvest years and releasing those stores when harvests were poor. Wang Mang abolished slavery once and for all.

However well intentioned Wang Mang's reform efforts, his reign soon ran into trouble because every reform that improved the lives of the peasants came at the expense of those with money and

A team of Chinese archaeologists unloads supplies at their excavation site in the Taklimakan Desert, which covers part of the Xinjiang Uygur Autonomous Region in northwestern China. In recent years, a host of exciting archaeological discoveries have helped scholars better understand the ancient history of China. One of the more surprising finds: that people with European origins may have occupied the Taklimakan Desert 4,000 years ago.

power. Even the lucrative trade on the Silk Road ground to a halt because traders refused to accept the bronze coins in place of gold.

It was too far, too fast. The nobles were on the verge of forcing Wang Mang to abdicate when nature did the job for them. Catastrophic floods of the Yellow River drowned thousands and turned millions more into refugees. Droughts followed. Convinced that Wang Mang did not, after all, have the Mandate of Heaven, the homeless peasants formed an organization called the Red Eyebrows Society and rose up in revolt. With help from the Huns of the north, relatives of the Han emperors joined forces with the peasants. In A.D. 23 they reached the capital and killed Wang Mang.

Wang Mang's reform experiment had failed, and the Han were once again supreme. Never again, until the revolutions in the 20th century, would the Han system of Confucian scholarship and civil service administration be seriously questioned. Wealthy families would continue refining the unique civilization of China in the arts and literature. Masses of peasants would struggle to eke out a tenuous living. Both the glories and the excesses of the Chinese Way were imprinted with the early Han and would continue intact for nearly 2,000 years.

Chronology

Ca. 10,000 B.C. The last Ice Age ends.

Ca. 5000 B.C. Agriculture first begins to develop in Neolithic China.

Ca. 2200 B.C. Crude early bronze objects made.

Ca. 2000–ca.1600 B.C. The Xia dynasty, once thought to be mythical, flourishes.

Ca. 1700–ca. 1027 B.C. Shang dynasty.

Ca. 1027–771 B.C. Western Zhou dynasty.

770 B.C. Following the overthrow of the Zhou king You, his successor flees eastward and establishes a new capital at Luoyang, inaugurating the Eastern Zhou era.

770–476 B.C. The Spring and Autumn period, which is marked by continual warfare among smaller states in the absence of a central authority.

475–221 B.C. The Warring States period, during which seven major states fight one another for supremacy.

221 B.C. The Qin state triumphs over its last remaining rivals, and Qin Shi Huang Di founds the first dynasty to rule over a unified China; guided by Legalist principles, the Qin dynasty rules repressively.

210 B.C. Qin Shi Huang Di dies.

206 B.C. The Qin dynasty is overthrown and the Han dynasty established; over the next 200 years of Han rule, state administration by Confucian scholars will be firmly established, the main characteristics of Chinese culture will emerge, and the Chinese empire will be expanded into Korea, Vietnam, and western China.

A.D. 9 The regent Wang Mang becomes emperor and begins a program of reforms designed to restore the financial health of the empire and improve the plight of peasants.

23 Following a period of natural disasters, Wang Mang is overthrown and killed by rebels; the Han dynasty is restored, setting the pattern for nearly two millennia of Chinese imperial governments to come.

Glossary

Confucianism—a philosophy espousing a hierarchy of mutual respect and responsibility, which became the dominant ideology of imperial China.

ding—a three-legged pot; the ancient Chinese king Yu created nine bronze *dings*, possession of which symbolized legitimate authority to rule.

dynasty—a family or group that maintains power for several generations; history is usually chronicled in China in terms of dynasties.

feudal—characteristic of a political system under which the lesser nobility pledged allegiance to (and in turn was protected by) a king, who distributed land to the nobility.

humanism —a mode of thinking involving human ideas, ideals, and values.

Legalism—the guiding philosophy of the Qin dynasty, which held that severe, certain punishment should be meted out for all transgressions, and rewards should be given for cooperation, regardless of an individual's social status or family connections.

Mandate of Heaven—the concept that the right to rule is divinely bestowed and will be taken from a bad ruler and awarded to one with more merit and virtue.

Neolithic—referring to the last period of the Stone Age (ca. 10,000–2500 B.C. in China) or to the cultures that existed during that time.

oracle bones—prepared animal bones or tortoise shells that were used in ancient China for divination, especially by the Shang.

shaman—a priest who communicates with spirits, usually while in a trance and often through animal totems.

Silk Road—the ancient set of trade routes linking China with the Middle East.

tamped earth—a building process whereby layers of earth are tamped hard to build strong, thick walls.

Taoism—a philosophy that, in broad terms, advocates harmony with the natural order and that had significant influence in imperial China.

taotie—a characteristic "monster mask" found on nearly all Shang bronze ritual vessels.

terra-cotta—a soft, reddish tan pottery.

vassal—an individual or lesser state owing allegiance to a feudal lord.

Further Reading

Bagley, Robert, ed. *Ancient Sichuan: Treasures from a Lost Civilization*. Seattle and Princeton, N.J.: Seattle Art Museum and Princeton University Press, 2001.

Blunden, Carolyn, and Mark Elvin. *Cultural Atlas of China* (rev. ed.). New York: Checkmark/Facts On File, 1998.

Lewis, Mark Edward. *The Early Chinese Empires: Qin and Han* (History of Imperial China). Cambridge, Mass.: Belknap Press of Harvard University Press, 2007.

Liu, Li, and Xingcan Chen. *State Formation in Early China*. London: Gerald Duckworth & Co., 2010.

Paludan, Ann. *Chronicle of the Chinese Emperors: The Reign-by-Reign Record of the Rulers of Imperial China*. London: Thames & Hudson, 1998.

Rubin, Vitaly A. *Individual and State in Ancient China: Essays on Four Chinese Philosophers*. New York: Columbia University Press, 1976.

Sawyer, Ralph D., translator. *The Seven Military Classics of Ancient China, Including "The Art of War."* Boulder, Colo.: Westview Press, 1993.

Schwartz, Benjamin I. *The World of Thought in Ancient China*. Cambridge, Mass.: Belknap Press of Harvard University Press, 1985.

Wills, John E., Jr. *Mountain of Fame: Portraits in Chinese History*. Princeton, N.J.: Princeton University Press, 1994.

Yuan, Gao. *Lure the Tiger Out of the Mountains: The 36 Stratagems of Ancient China*. New York: Simon & Schuster, 1991.

Internet Resources

http://www.mnsu.edu/emuseum/prehistory/china/index.html

This excellent site from Minnesota State University contains extensive information on China's dynasties, from Neolithic times to 1911.

http://www.metmuseum.org/toah/ht/02/eac/ht02eac.htm

A time line of Chinese history.

http://www.42explore2.com/china.htm

Information and links related to ancient China.

http://www.ancientchina.co.uk/menu.html

The British Museum's Web pages on ancient China offer information on a variety of topics, stunning photos, and fun interactive challenges.

http://www.historyforkids.org/learn/china/

This site, designed for middle school students, includes links to brief articles about topics such as art, architecture, food, philosophy, religion, and science in ancient China.

Index

Numbers in **bold italics** refer to captions.

Picture Credits

Contributors

SHEILA HOLLIHAN-ELLIOT is a popular writer on China. Fascinated with Chinese culture since she was a child and her father did business in the "Red China" of the 1950s, she has studied the history and arts of China and has spent time observing firsthand the enormous changes that are occurring in the country today. She also wrote the book *Art and Architecture of China* for this series. She graduated from Vassar College and is a member of The China Institute in New York City.

JIANWEI WANG, a native of Shanghai, received his B.A. and M.A. in international politics from Fudan University in Shanghai and his Ph.D. in political science from the University of Michigan. He is now the Eugene Katz Letter and Science Distinguished Professor and chair of the Department of Political Science at the University of Wisconsin–Stevens Point. He is also a guest professor at Fudan University in Shanghai and Zhongshan University in Guangzhou.

Professor Wang's teaching and research interests focus on Chinese foreign policy, Sino-American relations, Sino-Japanese relations, East Asia security affairs, UN peacekeeping operations, and American foreign policy. He has published extensively in these areas. His most recent publications include *Power of the Moment: America and the World After 9/11* (Xinhua Press, 2002), which he coauthored, and *Limited Adversaries: Post-Cold War Sino-American Mutual Images* (Oxford University Press, 2000).

Wang is the recipient of numerous awards and fellowships, including grants from the MacArthur Foundation, Social Science Research Council, and Ford Foundation. He has also been a frequent commentator on U.S.-China relations, the Taiwan issue, and Chinese politics for major news outlets.